CONTENTS

© Chancerel Publishers 1981

First published in this edition 1981 by
Octopus Books Limited
59, Grosvenor Street,
London W1.

Planned and created by
Chancerel Publishers Limited,
40, Tavistock Street,
London WC2E 7PB.

ISBN 0 7064 1553 1

Produced by Mandarin Publishers Limited,
22a Westland Road, Quarry Bay, Hong Kong.

Printed in Hong Kong

Origination by ReproSharp, London EC1
and La Cromolito, Milan.

Photographs

Allsport (Don Morley)   Page 6 (4), 72.
          (Tony Duffy)   Page 75.
John Shedden   Page 5, 9, 12, 16, 32, 34,
   41, 58.
Samas s.p.a.   Page 10
Transworld Feature Syndicate   Page 21.
J Allan Cash   Page 24, 56, 66.
Russel/Kelly Photography   Page 44, 71.
Jasper Partinon for Impressions   Page 47.
Norm Clasen   Page 51, 74.
Station des Arcs   Page 52.
Austrian Tourist Office   Page 63.
W. Kerstein   Page 65.
Fotogram (Deluc)   Page 68.
Swiss Tourist Office   Endpapers.

LET'S GO SKIING

**Text by Dennis Nelson
and Sally Gordon
Illustrations by Gerard Pestarque**

Above: *Franz Klammer (Austria); farmer's son, who trained with electronic sensors on his skis. Won Olympic gold medal for downhill in 1976 and many World Cup races.* Below: *Ken Read (Canada); from Calgary; top downhill skier, runner up in 1980 World Cup downhill; suffered injury in 1981.*

Above: *Ingemar Stenmark (Sweden); trains by cycling and tightrope walking; won Olympic slalom and giant slalom gold medals (1980) and over 60 World Cup races.* Below: *Marie Thérèse Nadig (Switz.); overall World Cup champion 1981; skis downhill and slalom.*

TO THE SLOPES

The right choice of how, when and where to go makes all the difference between magic and misery on your first ski holiday. Choose the right place, equipment and time of year and skiing will soon become a passion.

You may have read how some ski superstars began their skiing careers – but how can you begin yours? First you must travel to the slopes and there are numbers of ways of doing this. How you go is likely to depend on how close you are to a ski resort. Generally the cheapest (and a very cheerful!) way for a student is to join a school or college party. You could think about joining a ski club if there is one close by; they often organize holidays for members. Other possibilities are to book a holiday through a travel agent, or to go independently with family or friends.

In many cases the arrangements will be made through a tour operator who offers a *package deal*. Check the price carefully in this instance. It does not always include the *ski pack*, that is the cost of instruction, lift pass and hire of equipment, all of which can boost the price of the holiday considerably if you have not taken them into account.

If you have a choice of where to go, making up your mind can be very difficult. Many countries offer excellent skiing facilities, and how do you choose between them?

Price is usually a governing factor. Then, if you are a beginner, look for a resort that has plenty of open gentle nursery slopes to start you off on the right tracks. There are several other points you might like to consider:

● **The type of resort** Do you want to go to a traditional alpine village which has evolved into a ski resort, or to a modern complex that has sprung up purely as a centre for skiers?

● **When do you want to go?** At the beginning of the season (early Winter) and at the end of the season (late Spring) choose a high resort that will have early snowfalls and retain its snow later into the year. The price will be affected; tour operators offer *low-season* and *high-season* prices.

● **What sort of accommodation do you want?** An hotel, chalet or apartment? Whichever you choose, make sure it is not too far away from the major ski areas. A long walk in uncomfortable boots can be discouraging, and a ride in a special bus an added expense.

● **Are you interested in the apres-ski life?** If so, check what the resort offers. Established villages may have special local activities – fondue parties, folk-dance evenings as well as toboganning, ice skating and curling (bowls on ice). Some purpose-built resorts have only discos; some have every facility.

How can I prepare for skiing?

Skiing is fast, dynamic and physical. It makes great demands on the body, asking for strong muscles and a high level of **fitness.** The fitter you are the more you will enjoy skiing and the better you will be at it. Nobody acquires the necessary strength and fitness overnight though; plan a routine of daily exercise and follow it for three months before your holiday.

General fitness comes through regular active exercise, such as cycling, jogging, swimming – even daily skipping or running on the spot. But you must acquire **specific ski fitness** too. This means exercising and strengthening the main muscles that will be used in skiing, so that the joints that take the principal stresses – such as the ankles and knees – will be thoroughly strengthened.

The exercises illustrated on this page will help you to acquire the necessary strength and flexibility in your muscles and joints. Build up your fitness programme gradually; go at it too vigorously at the outset and you might tear or pull a muscle or ligament unnecessarily.

There is nothing like going skiing to acquire ski fitness. If the mountains are on your doorstep, then this presents no problem – at least in the winter. But what of places where there are no mountains? Many of these cater for the skier with **artificial ski slopes.** On these you can learn

---

Cycling, jogging, skipping and running on the spot are all good ski-preparation exercises. You should start training about three months before you go. Below right: Certain isometric exercises are important for specific ski fitness.

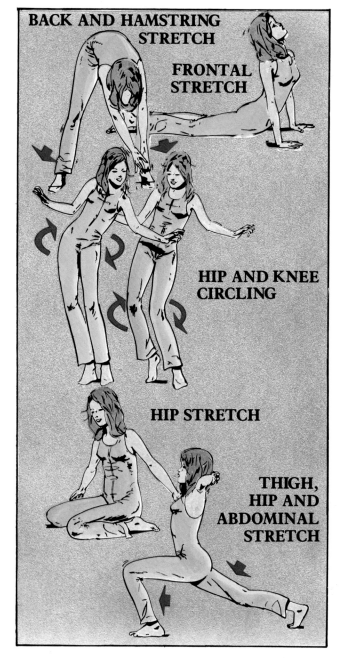

BACK AND HAMSTRING STRETCH

FRONTAL STRETCH

HIP AND KNEE CIRCLING

HIP STRETCH

THIGH, HIP AND ABDOMINAL STRETCH

Competive action on the Pontypool, Wales, dry ski slope. Artificial slopes, made of nylon bristles, are excellent for training before a ski holiday.

What do I wear?

Skiers wear special clothes, not as you might imagine so that they look fashionable and attractive, but in order to keep them warm at all times. We ski in places where there are extremes of temperature and weather conditions. For example, the further you go up a mountain the colder it becomes. It is essential, therefore, to wear clothes that will protect you from wind and cold.

Outer Clothes This could be an all-in-one suit, an anorak worn with special ski trousers (made from heavy duty, elasticated material, padded on the knees) or an anorak worn with salopettes (trousers made from stretch or quilted synthetic material, usually in a dungaree design).

These exercises will make you ski-fit. Leg and stomach muscles particularly need strengthening. Ski fitness helps you avoid accidents.

SQUAT JUMPS

SQUAT THRUSTS

REVERSE ARM PRESS-UPS

SIT-UPS

and practise many of the techniques of skiing that you would otherwise have to learn when you arrive at the snow.

Artificial ski slopes are generally made of a carpet of nylon bristles arranged in a diamond pattern and laid over a slope. The surface is similar to snow, except that it has greater friction. In a course of instruction on dry ski slopes – say, six two-hour lessons – you can learn just about all the technical manoeuvres you would learn in a week's skiing at a resort.

Having learnt to ski on an artificial slope, you will find there will be a slight period of adjustment when you first ski on snow, as you discover the differences in sliding and how the general terrain affects the momentum of your skis.

Don't worry – you will soon get used to the way in which your skis slide so much more easily on the snow.

Whichever you choose, look for outer clothes that are **windproof, water resistant** (rather than waterproof), and made of anti-gliss fabric (to stop you sliding on the snow). Ideally, they should be washable too.

Pale colours – white and cream – may look attractive in the shop, but they will quickly become grubby. Bright reds, blues and greens are more practical and in fact, against the snowy background, they look smarter, too. Ski clothes made from quilted material will be the warmest. An important part to keep warm, incidentally, is the area around your kidneys often left unprotected by a short anorak, so choose an anorak that is long enough. It should overlap your ski

Ski clothing is constantly changing in fashion, but not in function. Above all it should be warm.

trousers by at least 10-15cm (4-6ins). Waist-length anoraks may look neat, but they are not very practical. Look for one which has a high close-fitting collar and close-fitting cuffs and bottom; it will keep out the snow at all times. Ordinary anoraks are not usually warm enough for skiing.

Hats and gloves Always wear a hat (preferably woollen) even if the day looks warm and sunny; a surprising amount of heat is lost through the head. Mittens or gloves are essential to protect hands and keep them warm. Mittens are usually warmer than gloves, but gloves give a greater range of movement and a better grip on the ski poles. If you want to wear gloves, but find them cold, wear some silk inner gloves, too.

Socks You should not need to wear more than one pair of warm ski socks; choose three-quarter length cotton or wool ones. If your feet are cold, wear a pair of silk socks too (not extra woolly ones).

Under clothes A thin cotton or wool polo-neck pullover and a thicker woollen sweater are the ideal clothes to wear under your outer ski garments. Wear a vest, or better still, thermal underwear (now widely available) to keep you warm, rather than pile on more jumpers. These will be bulky and will restrict your arms.

Goggles and glasses A tremendous glare reflects off the snow, particularly in sunny weather. This will soon make your eyes sore and give you headaches unless you wear goggles or sunglasses. Sunglasses are more comfortable and more practical, but buy those made of flexible plastic, that will not splinter if you fall on them. If you wear spectacles, goggles can be useful to hold them on.

Boots The developments in modern skiing techniques have led to great improvements and variations in ski boots. Modern boots are made from a plastic shell with a removable inner boot. Although they vary considerably in quality, all are infinitely more comfortable and supportive than the old leather skiing boots. The inner boot comprises a thin plastic shoe with foam inside. This moulds when the foot is placed in it, so it assumes the shape of the individual foot. The quality of the moulding can be refined still further, according to the quality of the boot, and it accounts for the greater comfort of ski boots today. Bear in mind that hired boots, particu-

Modern plastic ski boots with clips. The angle of the back forces the lower leg forward at the ankle.

larly at the end of a season, may not be all that comfortable, as they will already have moulded to the shape of other people's feet. Modern boots have varying numbers of clips; current thinking is to reduce the number as far as possible, so ultra-modern boots have only one or – at the most – two clips.

Skis As with boots, developments in both recreational and racing ski techniques, have led to developments and changes in ski design. There is no perfect ski for all types of skiing. Skiers have to choose skis that are suitable for their standard of skiing and the type of snow and terrain they will ski on. Skis vary in length, design and flex pattern – that is how they react to the pressure and stresses put on them. Novice skiers will be looking for **mid-length** or **compact skis** of a suitable height (see next page).

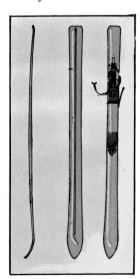

Right: *Skis are slightly concave. This is called camber. It allows them to flex.*
Left: *The main parts of a ski. The tip is called the shovel; the heel is the tail; the underside is the sole; the centre is the waist; the tracking groove runs down the sole.*

11

YOUR FIRST DAY

On your first day you need to gain confidence, learn to balance and master your skis.
The green, beginners' slopes are the place for you to practise during the first few days.

With all that preparation behind you, at last you are ready for the snow! But what must you do to begin skiing? Well, if you do not have all your own equipment, you must go to the ski shop at the resort and hire it. Alternatively, you can hire everything at home and bring it with you.

Boots Ask for a boot in your size (find out your equivalent continental or American size), and undo the clips. Make sure there are no foreign bodies inside, pull the tongue right out, then put your foot into it. Tap your heel down, then do up the clips so they are comfortable and supportive, but not too tight. Stand up and see if you can lift up your heel inside the boot. If you are able to move your heel considerably, and you can not stop this by tightening the clips, try a smaller size. You should not be able to move your heel more than 1cm ($\frac{1}{2}$in). Now stand on your toes; your foot should not slide forwards. Don't expect the boots to feel instantly comfortable; they are bound to feel constricting.

Skis Your skiing ability, combined with your height and weight, will determine the type and length of ski you should have. If you have skied before, you will have some idea of the sort you want. A beginner should look for mid-length, or compact skis, around chin or eye height.

Safety bindings These are the safety release

mechanisms that hold your feet in the skis, but which should release when necessary – such as in a fall. But no binding is one hundred per cent fail

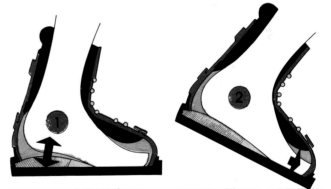

Above and right; *It is important that your boots are the right size and that your skis are the right height for you. Check the fit of the boots when the clips are done up. Your heel should hardly move and your toe should not slide forwards. Skis should be between chin and eye height.*

Left: *This is a step-in safety binding. It consists of a toe piece, which releases sideways, and a heel piece, which releases upwards and forwards. It is important to have your bindings checked by an expert to make sure they are correctly adjusted, so that they release in a fall.*

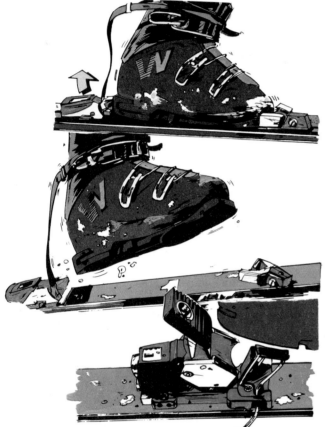

Above: *Retaining straps (top) or ski stoppers (bottom) prevent skis running away from you after a fall. Run-away, rogue skis can kill, so make sure your retaining straps are fastened.*

Right: *The correct way to grip ski poles, Insert your hand upwards through the wrist thong. Then close your fingers around both the thong and the pole grip.*

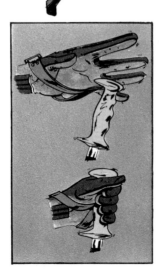

safe, particularly in a slow, spiralling fall.

Many types of binding are available, but they fall into two basic categories: **step-in** or **automatic,** and **semi-automatic.** Most release in three directions (see above). The pressure on the binding needs to be great enough to hold the foot firm in normal skiing manoeuvres, but not so great that it will not release before forces are applied which could cause a bone to break. To ensure this, **bindings must be checked by an expert,** who will know if they are set correctly.

You can make a crude check yourself by swivelling the toe piece using the heel of your hand. If you can move it easily, it is too loose. If you cannot move it at all, it's probably too tight. Try these tests, too:

1. Put one foot in the binding: kick the side front of that boot with your other foot sharply. You should be able to kick the foot out.

2. Put your feet in the bindings and ask a friend to stand on the front of your skis. Lean back and jerk forward sharply with your heels. Your bindings should release.

Remember that these tests are only a rough indication. An expert check is essential.

Ski stoppers If your feet are to be released from the skis when you fall, there must be some way of ensuring that your skis stay close by you. Runaway skis that go flying down the mountain are extremely dangerous to other skiers (they could easily kill someone) and, of course, you may lose them altogether if they fly over a precipice. The two means of stopping skis after a fall, are to wear **retaining straps** (straps attached to the back of the binding, which fasten round your ankles), or to fit **ski brakes** or **stoppers** to the ski (see diagram). Ski stoppers should stop the ski in its tracks; retaining straps mean the ski will stay attached to you and in a heavy fall this can be dangerous as the skis could strike your head or body.

Ski poles Beginners use ski poles chiefly to help them balance on their skis. Soon you will use them for changing direction on the slope – when you are slope-hanging (see page 20). Later on, they will help you to turn. For pole length, stand up straight, put the pole tip on your ski in front of the binding. Grip the handle – your forearm should be level with ground.

Is it easy to walk in ski boots?

The short answer to this is, no! Or at least, walking may be easy, but it is not comfortable. Ski boots are not made for walking, so try to avoid it. If, for example, you have quite a long walk to the slopes from your hotel, wear ordinary snow boots and carry your ski boots. Change over in the café closest to the lift or slope you are using.

If you do have to walk a little way in ski boots, experiment to find out what is most comfortable for you. Some people find it most comfortable to do up all the clips quite tightly; others prefer to loosen them completely. A word of warning: walking in ski boots can cause your ankles to swell and give you blisters. Either could cause you great discomfort, and maybe stop you from skiing for a day or so. You can also damage boots by walking in them too much.

The diagrams below show you how to carry your skis. Fasten them together with the ski straps (this stops them slipping) and rest them on your shoulder with the tips pointing down and the heels high. Make sure you are not going to hit anyone when you turn round. You will find, incidentally, that it is much more comfortable if you rest the flat part of the skis against your shoulder, rather than the edges.

If you have to carry your skis a long way, it is easiest of all to use the poles to make a carrying handle as shown in the diagram, and carry your skis like a suitcase. To do this, put the skis together (using the ski straps again), then place the poles end to end, looping the handles over the tips and heels of the skis.

Can I start to ski now?

You can, but never on your own. No beginner should take to the slopes by himself, even if he has learnt to ski on an artificial slope. It is dangerous, at least until you have the feel of the snow. Never be tempted to teach yourself how to ski, you will quickly fall into bad habits and adopt incorrect techniques, which are very difficult to change later.

All resorts have at least one **ski school**. The skiing techniques and methods of teaching will vary from country to country, although you will

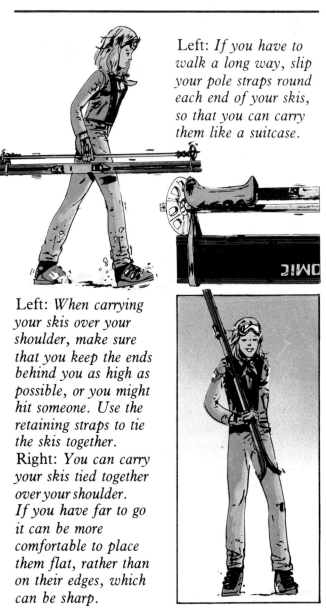

Left: *If you have to walk a long way, slip your pole straps round each end of your skis, so that you can carry them like a suitcase.*

Left: *When carrying your skis over your shoulder, make sure that you keep the ends behind you as high as possible, or you might hit someone. Use the retaining straps to tie the skis together.*
Right: *You can carry your skis tied together over your shoulder. If you have far to go it can be more comfortable to place them flat, rather than on their edges, which can be sharp.*

find that at the top echelons of skiing, techniques vary very little.

When you join the ski school at your resort, you will be assessed by an instructor to see which class you should join. Ski schools cater for all standards of skier from the very beginners to the very advanced. Usually there are six graded classes, and each should have ten to twelve people. If there are more than twelve in your class, it is getting crowded. At fifteen – complain! This is too many pupils for one instructor to teach properly – and you are paying.

Watch and listen to your instructor very carefully. He should be able to speak your language. Try and stay close to him so that you can see exactly what he is doing. Then it will be easier to copy him.

Private instruction is usually very expensive, but it can be very worthwhile. If you are having trouble mastering some particular technique, private lessons could be the answer.

So, you've joined your class and the time has come to put on your skis. Your instructor will take you to a flat area of snow, where you can do this without any danger of your skis sliding down the hill.

Place the skis parallel to each other on the snow, turning one on its side. Put your poles close by, too. Make sure the bottom of your boot is free from snow, using your ski pole to clear away any snow packed onto the sole, as shown in the diagram. Check that the clips on your boots are done up tightly and then open the safety release binding on the ski if it is not open already. Position your foot squarely on the ski stepping into the binding, then press down to snap it shut. Now put on the other ski in the same way; remember to clear the snow away from the bottom of the boot first.

My skis feel so strange!

Wearing skis for the first time is like having feet that are six or seven times longer than the ones you are used to! So the first thing to do is to get used to the way they feel by trying some **basic awareness exercises.**

Try rocking backwards and forwards on the skis. Can you feel the support your boots are giving you? Bend your ankles forward and lift the heel of one ski, keeping the tip on the ground. Put it down and try the same thing with the other ski. Then lean back slightly and lift each tip in turn. Now lift up the whole ski keeping it level. Then try lifting one ski and tapping its tip on either side of the other one.

Without picking up your skis, slide them backwards and forwards alternatively over the

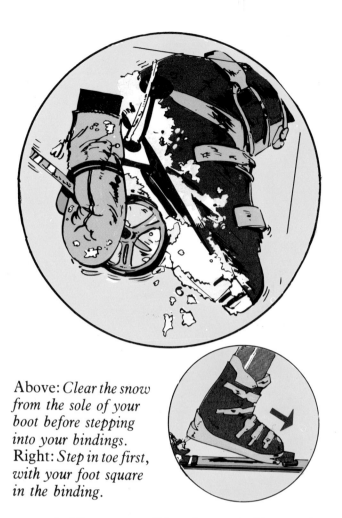

Above: *Clear the snow from the sole of your boot before stepping into your bindings.*
Right: *Step in toe first, with your foot square in the binding.*

ground. Now try walking forward. You can't really walk in the normal way; instead you must keep the skis parallel and flat on the ground and shuffle or slide them forward. Don't lift your feet, but press your knees forwards towards the tips of the skis. Use your ski poles to help push you along, keeping the pole tips behind your feet. Think about keeping your skis flat on the ground as you move; it will be far harder if you try to lift them.

How do I turn round?

To turn round in order to change direction, you have to pivot on the tips of your skis and lift your heels around. Or you can pivot on the heels and lift the tips around. The first time, try pivoting on the tips.

Start with your skis together, then just follow the movement shown in the diagram overleaf. Step out one heel so that your skis are in a V-shape. Bring the other ski alongside. Repeat these movements, pivoting on your ski tips, until you have turned your skis completely and are facing in the opposite direction.

Now try to turn back to face the way you were pointing first, by pivoting on your heels. This time, lean back slightly and lift your foot up

Awareness exercises will help you overcome the strange feeling of wearing skis for the first time.

towards the top of your boots. This will automatically lift up the tip of your ski and you can then swing it out into the V-shape. Practise by making full, 360° turns in both directions using both methods. This turn is known as a **clock turn** or a **step turn.**

When you feel quite confident, how about a test of co-ordination? Try a **star turn;** this is a turn in which you link the heel and tip pivoting movements. In other words, take your first step by moving your heels and pivoting on your tips, followed by a step in which you pivot on your heels and move your toes. Work round in a complete circle; now look at the star pattern your skis have left on the snow.

It won't take you long to feel quite at home with your skis. But, before you can actually take to the slope to begin skiing, you should learn

Above: *Try not to lift your skis when walking forwards. Instead just shuffle them along the ground.*
Right: *Use the clock turn to change direction. Start with your skis together. Pivot the left ski on its tip and step out in a V-shape. Bring the right ski alongside. Repeat until you are facing in the opposite direction.*
Below: *The fall line is the line of least resistance from top to bottom of a hill.*

something about hills.

All slopes have an imaginary line from top to bottom, which is the line of least resistance. This is a path that a free moving body, such as a ball or a stream of water, would follow down the hill. This line is commonly called the **fall line.** It will not always be a straight line from top to bottom, as it must change direction as the direction of the slope changes.

How do I step up the slope?

The fall line is important when you come to step up a slope, for in order to progress uphill in the way that you want to – that is without taking one step up and six down – it is necessary to take up position directly *across the fall line*. This means being at right angles to it.

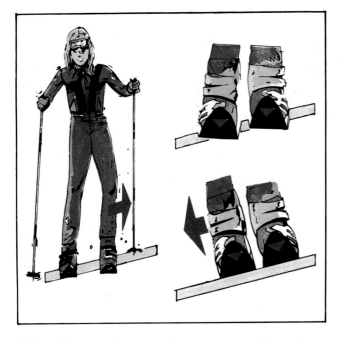

When side-stepping up a slope, set your skis on their edges, so that they dig into the snow and provide a grip. If they are flat on the surface of the snow they will simply slip down the hill.

The herringbone is an alternative way to climb up a slope. Face uphill in the fall line, making a V-shape with your skis. Bend your knees and press them inwards to grip with the inside edges of the skis.

Place the skis parallel about 60cm (12ins) apart with the top ski slightly ahead. Turn the skis on to their uphill edges, so that these bite into the slope. This you do by gently pressing your knees and hips uphill, although at the same time you must keep your knees and upper body bent forwards.

Biting the edges into the hill this way provides you with a platform from which to push up and walk up the slope. Be conscious of standing on the big toe of your lower foot and the little toe of your upper foot. Now take a step uphill with the leading (uphill) foot, by pushing off the instep of the lower (downhill) foot. Maintain an awareness of standing on **edged skis** – that is with the uphill edges turned into the slope – or else you may begin to slide down the hill. Once you have placed the uphill ski up the slope, push off your lower foot to bring this ski alongside the uphill ski; the movement should be so sharp, maintaining weight and balance over the lower foot all the time.

Climbing up hill is the first time you have used your edges. Their application is so fundamental to skiing that you should try to learn good **edge sense** right from the start. Improve this sense by **side shuffling** down the slope.

Side shuffling is done by maintaining your position across the fall line and pushing the skis sideways against the upper edges. Press against the edge of your lower ski to force it downwards.

Keep your body weight and balance over it and draw the upper ski down alongside. Keep feeling an awareness of pressure on the little toe of your upper foot to maintain the correct edge.

Speed up the action, making small shuffling movements with your skis whilst moving continuously sideways.

Can I ski down the slope now?

At last you are ready for your first slide downhill. Now you must develop your balance, finding the best posture to keep you on your feet. Make up your mind to be very relaxed before you set off. Skiing is fun, after all.

Skiing down the fall line is called **schussing** or **straight running**. As you become more proficient, you will find schussing the most exhilarating – and simplest – of all ski movements.

Success in your first schuss depends largely on starting from a good position. First, change your grip on the ski poles, holding them as shown in the top diagram overleaf. Feel the end of the pole in the heel of your hand. Then with your skis still across the fall line, plant your poles, directly downhill of the ski tips, so they are about shoulder width apart. Keep your arms straight locking your elbows to support your weight, and simply do a clock turn (pivoting your toes, stepping out with your heels) until you are facing downhill.

Left: *Having climbed the slope, you must turn to face downhill, ready for your first run. Support your weight on your poles and do a clock turn. This is called slope hanging. Use only on gentle slopes.*

Below left: *You are now ready to schuss or run straight down the hill. This is one of the easiest of ski movements, and one of the most exhilarating.*

Left: *For a good schuss posture, your shoulders should be slightly rounded and relaxed; arms should be forward; ankles, knees and hips should be slightly flexed; your weight should be balanced comfortably over the balls of the feet.*

You are now **slope-hanging** – that is pointing downhill, supporting yourself with your arms pushing on your poles. Your skis are pointing downhill between your poles. They should be flat on the snow, parallel, about 20-25cm (8-10ins) apart at the tips. Allow your knees, ankles and upper body to bend very slightly in a relaxed manner, and be aware that your weight is on the balls of your feet. Then just relax, slowly releasing the poles and flexing your wrist as you move forward, so that the poles point backwards, as in the picture. Let yourself slide down the hill with your sticks behind you. Do not attempt to do anything to stop – just let the terrain slow you down and eventually stop naturally. Now climb up the hill and run down again.

Your posture is very important. But become accustomed to the feel of sliding downhill before worrying too much about it. As you gain confidence, your balance will become better and your posture will improve naturally. Use the follow-

ing points to check how close you are to a relaxed, controlled posture:
● Your shoulders should be relaxed and gently rounded.
● Your arms need to be held forward in an easy way with your hands about hip high.
● Your hips, knees and ankles should be slightly flexed, ready to absorb any bumps or hollows in the terrain.
● Can you feel where your weight is on your feet? It should be balanced evenly over the balls of your feet.

Will I fall over?

Probably – one thing in skiing is certain; you are likely to fall sometime during your first day! Everybody does, but actually it's all part of the fun. Just get up and try again.

If you feel yourself falling – don't fight it. If a fall is inevitable, it is best to let yourself go so that you fall in as relaxed a fashion as you can.

When you feel that you have lost your balance try to sit down uphill and to the side of your skis. Try not to put your hands out to break your fall – it is much better to let the tougher, better padded parts of your body take the impact. As you land, try to stretch and straighten your legs, so they are pointing straight out beneath you. Learning to fall like this will help you to avoid injury.

Getting up after a fall can be rather more trying than the fall itself. After removing all the snow from down your neck and up your sleeves, position your skis downhill across the fall line. Do this *before* you attempt to push yourself up on to your feet. Shuffle your behind down towards the skis, so that you are sitting as close as possible to the bindings. Bend your upper body forwards over the front of the skis and push yourself up with your uphill arm. Move into an upright position with a forwards and sideways rocking motion, moving your weight over on to your feet.

If you fall in the soft snow just off the piste (see page 69), you will find that you need fierce determination to stand on your feet again. The best way is to pack down the snow around your skis first; then push yourself up from your ski poles laid flat and crossed on the snow by your side.

If your skis come off in a fall, pick yourself and your skis up as quickly as you can and move to the side of the slope, out of the way of others in the class who are skiing behind you.

You must always put the lower or downhill ski on first: incline it on its uphill edge, pushing it into the snow if you can to make a platform. Make sure the bottom of your boot is free of snow, then step into the binding. Transfer your weight to the downhill ski, brush the snow off your other boot and step into the uphill ski.

Learning to fall correctly can prevent injury.

Develop balance and confidence

What you do now is practise, and keep practising, for the important thing at this stage of learn-

Left: *As you fall, sit back and straighten your legs. Keep your hands clear, in front of you. Everyone falls to start with. It is part of skiing and generally brings nothing more serious than a laugh. Above all, do not fight a fall.*

Right: *Before standing up place your skis below you across the fall line to stop them sliding down the slope. In soft snow place your poles on the snow and use them to push yourself up.*

Learning to ski very young is a great advantage.

ing to ski is to develop your balance until you are as confident as you can be about keeping it. Relaxed posture is essential for good balance; a relaxed posture is essential if you are to become a good skier. And the better the skier you are, the more you will enjoy yourself.

The sliding movement of a schuss is likely to be something that feels alien to you; after all the only time you really come across such a feeling is when you are skiing. Practise your schuss over lots of different types of ground and make it fun by playing games with the others in your class. Try doing all or some of the following exercises as you ski:

- Crouch down low on your skis, then stand up very tall.
- Drop a glove halfway up the slope as you climb it; then pick it up as you ski down.
- Put a balloon between your knees at the top of the slope and ski down with it remaining in position (this helps to ensure that your knees are the same distance apart as your skis – which they should be).
- Position some ski poles down the hill, in such a way that you have to crouch down to ski

underneath them.

- Devise some relay races to play with the others.
- Rock forwards and backwards on your skis.
- Shuffle your skis backwards and forwards as you slide down the hill.

More will be said later about skiing over bumps, but at the moment, just try to remain relaxed. Keep your upper body still and look where you are going. Flex your knees and ankles as you rise over the bumps and use your legs as a form of suspension – like shock absorbers.

If you feel insecure at this stage, as if you are always just about to topple over, position your skis slightly wider apart, say about 45-60cm (18ins-2ft). The wider base this gives you will give you greater stability, and thus quickly increase your confidence. Remember though that your knees must be the same distance apart as your skis, otherwise it is impossible to keep your skis flat on the snow.

Crouching lower on your skis can also help to make you feel more secure. What this does is to lower your centre of gravity. And the lower your centre of gravity, the harder it is to fall over. Remember when you crouch lower on your skis though, that you must bend your ankles and not just your knees. Always feel that your weight is over the balls of your feet.

Besides bumpy terrain, ski also on slopes of different gradients, looking now for those that are a little steeper, so that you ski that little bit faster. Nothing changes when you ski faster; your position remains the same. Always make sure at this stage that there is a counter slope to the one you are skiing down, so that the opposite hill will automatically bring you to a stop.

What to do after skiing?

When you return to your hotel or chalet, the first thing to do is to take off your boots! If snow has found its way into them during the day, perhaps when you fell, making them wet, take out the inner linings and put them somewhere warm to dry. It really is important to start off the day with warm, dry boots.

Once into some other clothes, you will doubtless make for the local café for a hot drink. Plenty of drinks will help replace moisture lost in the exertion of skiing. Sugary cakes will help give you energy. Try to avoid living it up on the first night of your holiday. Even if you have not expended that much energy, you will be tired. Better to have an early night tonight to put you into good shape for tomorrow's skiing.

Above: *Just balancing on skis is not good enough, if you want to make progress. Develop dynamic balance by crouching, touching your toes and then standing up, while schussing downhill. Such exercises are designed to help you relax on your skis.*
Below: *Children learn quickly through play.*

YOUR FIRST WEEK

With one week's experience you should be able to ski with safety and control. If you learn the basic skills in this chapter you should be able to tackle the blue standard runs, higher up the mountain.

Your first day's skiing is behind you. No doubt you feel infinitely more confident now, than you did yesterday.

Before you put on those skis though, do a few exercises to **warm up your muscles.** Swing each arm round in a circle, alternately; bend down and touch your toes, then really stretch up high into the air; bend from the waist to either side, then twist to either side from the waist, turning your body to left and right. By now you should be tingling!

The first manoeuvring technique a skier learns is **snow ploughing.** This is the basis of good skiing technique. Learning to snow plough well will give you a firm foundation for future skiing movements. It is actually possible to learn to ski parallel by developing good snow ploughing techniques, as you will see later on.

What is a snow plough?

The snow plough is so called because of the position of the skis – they are positioned in a V-shape, like the blades of a plough. To understand the snow plough technique, think of a farmer ploughing the land. The blades of the

plough dig into the ground and push the earth to either side.

Although the ultimate aim of a snow plough in skiing is to change direction and to choose the line you take down a slope, it is necessary first, to learn to snow plough down the fall line, and to control the speed of the skis. Snow ploughing down the fall line is known as **snow plough gliding** and **braking.**

The snow plough glide first then; climb up the slope in the usual way, then face the fall line supporting your weight on your poles. Push your skis out into a V-shape from the tips to the heels, positioning them on their inside edges. The tips of your skis should be at least 7.5-10cm (3-4ins) apart and the heels should be very wide apart. The fall line should be in the centre of your skis and your weight should be placed evenly on each ski so they oppose each other equally. Say to yourself, **"equal weight, equal edge, equal pressure with the feet".** If any of these things are not equal, one ski will necessarily be dominant, which it should not be.

To glide down the slope in a snow plough, relax the pressure on your poles – just as you did before when schussing – and let yourself go.

Stand quite tall on your skis, but relaxed, and feel your weight on the balls of your feet, pressing on the big toe of both feet. In this way you will maintain that inside edge on your skis.

Practise a few glides like this, growing used to the feel of the action; then try a few stationary exercises to improve your glide. Stand at the bottom of the slope:

● Hop the back of the skis out into the snow plough position.
● Stand at the bottom of the slope in a schuss position with your weight well forward on the balls of your feet. Press on the big toes of both feet and push the backs of the skis out into a snow plough, pivoting on the tips.
● Now try the same sort of thing coming downhill; start off in a schuss with your skis flat and quite far apart. Now push the heels out into a snow plough as you slide down hill, then bring them together again into the schuss position. Select a slope and practise this a few times, seeing how many times you can go from a schuss to a snow plough and back to a schuss.

How do I brake in a snow plough?

In order to control your speed still more than you can in a snow plough glide, you will need to apply a greater braking effect on your skis. This you achieve by widening the V-shape and by

It is important to distribute your weight evenly on both skis. They should skid down the slopes against their inner edges.

Snow ploughing is the simplest means of controlling your skis on a gentle slope. The skis are placed in a V-shape. This is a gliding snow plough.

pressing harder on the inside edges of the skis whilst adopting a lower body stance. Think of a **braking snow plough** as just that – a means of *braking*, rather than stopping.   Start off in a gliding position, then press down on your skis feeling the pressure on the balls of your feet. Push on the inside edges of the skis, so as to widen the V-position. Allow your weight to come *very slightly backwards* on to the whole of your foot, so you can push down and out against your heels. As the skis widen, you will feel a braking effect.

Try refining both this action and your gliding snow plough by starting from the top of a hill in a glide, sinking down and pushing out into a braking action, coming back up to a glide, going down to a brake, and so on. Feel confident with that? Then try starting from a schuss, going to a glide, to a brake, to a schuss, glide, brake. Now try going straight to a schuss from a brake, without the glide. Sink down when you brake, stand high in the schuss.

You may find that your knees knock together when snow ploughing; try to avoid it – it makes the inside edges of the skis dig into the snow, causing the tips to cross. Feel your knees pushing forwards towards the ski tips, not inwards towards each other. When you go from a high stance to a low stance, bend at the ankles and hips as well as the knees. Practise gliding down the hill, shifting your position from high, to mid

If you are moving too fast in a snow plough glide, you can reduce speed by pushing down and out against your heels, to push the skis wider apart.

(normal) to low and back to high again, without ever altering the angle of the plough.

You will have noticed the words **high stance** and **low stance** above. Your stance on your skis varies according to the manoeuvre you are doing. In a snow plough glide, you should stand fairly high – that is standing tall, but relaxed on your skis. In a braking snow plough, you adopt a much lower stance.

You can improve your snow plough glide by making an outward, brushing action with your skis. Let your skis glide in a narrow V-shape. Then sink down and push out your heels to create a braking effect. Now try to become more versatile— try gliding in a low crouch, with your skis in a narrow V; straighten up again, pushing your skis out. Feel the pressure on the inside edges.

How do I turn the skis?

Learning to turn the skis in a snow plough is the final manoeuvre that will enable you to steer a course across the slope, moving in whichever direction you like. The skills you have learnt in the snow plough glide and brake will help you in the **snow plough turn.**

Let's turn to the left. Start in a glide down the fall line (remember – equal weight, equal edge, equal pressure); now feel an *awareness* of applying pressure with the big toe of your right foot. *Do nothing else* – don't change your position on the skis or alter the pressure on the left ski; you will begin to turn to the left. As long as you continue applying pressure on the big toe of the right foot, you will continue to turn, until you have turned so far that your skis will stop. Climb up the slope again and try a turn to the right – feeling the pressure on the big toe of the *left* foot.

When you feel you are beginning to master this means of turning, you can begin to improve the efficiency of the turn by applying a greater pressure with the inside of your foot and actually *turning* your foot in the direction of the turn. This is known as foot steering.

Start off in a glide again. As you apply the pressure on the big toe of your turning foot, increase the ankle and knee bend and *turn* your foot in the direction of your turning ski, whilst pressing your knee forward. The thing to remember is that the greater the pressure you apply on that turning ski, the more efficient the turn will be.

27

Snow plough pie

The temptation as you learn new, or more refined, aspects of a basic manoeuvre, is to change the original components of that manoeuvre – that is those you have already learnt. Think of the snow plough as a pie in which you have a number of basic ingredients. The basic ingredients of a snow plough are:

● Skis positioned in a V-shape from toe to heels.
● Skis placed equally on their inside edges.
● Equal weight with your feet, giving equal brushing pressure.

To turn the pie into a snow plough turn, you simply add one more ingredient:

● Steering the turning ski.

As ever, the path to improvement lies in practise and you can stop this from becoming boring by doing some exercises and games.

● Start off in a snow plough, then sink down and push one knee forward with your hand. Apply pressure with the big toe of the foot and keep your hand behind your knee as you turn.

In order to do a snow plough turn, all you have to do is steer your skis. Apply pressure to the big toe of your right foot and you will turn smoothly to the left.

● Now try some **snow plough garlands**. A garland is a series of turns, but only in one direction. It is a very useful skiing exercise – one that you can use when you come on to more advanced methods of turning, too. Start off in a high stance snow plough glide; sink down whilst applying pressure on your right ski. Let your skis turn to the left; stand up equally weighting both skis into a snow plough glide and repeat the action until you feel a continuous, strong up and down rhythm. Look at the marks your skis have left coming down the slopes – you will see why the exercise is called a garland. Of course, you should try doing it both ways; never practise turning to just one side – it will inevitably be the way you find the easiest.

Can I link turns in either direction?

Indeed you can, and when you can do so successfully *you can ski!* Just think – then you will be able to control where you go across the slope.

In fact, you were linking turns in the snow plough garland exercise above, but then they were linked in one direction. To link them to left and right, glide down the fall line, apply a down and forward motion on to the right ski to turn to the left and steer the ski round the turn. Let your body rise into a high stance so you can equalize the pressure over both skis and turn back into the fall line, as you did in the garland, then apply the down and forward motion on the left ski to turn right.

Think of linking turns in terms of skiing in the fall line and out of the fall line. To execute good linked turns, you need good rhythmic movement with a high stance in the fall line and a low stance, combined with a downward pressure as you turn. The efficiency of the turn depends on the quality of the steering. Try this exercise in fall line skiing to improve both the rhythm and the steering action.

Start off in a glide in the fall line and apply a short sharp pressure to one ski. As soon as you start to turn, stop applying the pressure, equalize your weight and balance over your skis by coming up in the fall line, and *immediately* apply short sharp pressure on the other ski. You will be turning quickly in and out of the fall line.

Now try changing the arc to make the turn more rounded so that it takes you much further across the fall line in either direction. This you do simply by applying pressure on to the turning ski for a longer period of time. Accompany it still with a good steering action – and you can now ski across the slope, picking the route of your choice.

Now that you can ski, the slopes you have been on will almost certainly be too short. As soon as you are proficient at skiing with linked snow plough turns, you can begin to go higher up the mountain – to explore new slopes. But make sure you stick to the easy ones – there is still a surprising amount to learn!

It is important for you to venture on to longer slopes now, for the way to improve your skiing is to practise over varied terrain, skiing for as long as possible in one run, and adapting all the manoeuvres that are now familiar to you.

How do I go higher up the mountain?

You take a lift – climbing would take far too long and would be far too strenuous. And you would be a nuisance to skiers coming down the slope. The first lift you will ride is a **drag lift** of some kind, and there are various types. The two you are most likely to encounter are the button lift and the T-bar.

Riding a drag lift is easy, but before you begin, try this exercise with a friend – and be prepared to laugh a lot! One of you take off your skis and put them on the ground. That person then holds out a ski pole to the other person who takes hold of it. The person wearing no skis then pulls his friend along over the snow; it will give you the feel of being pulled along – the sensation you will have on the drag lift.

Riding the button

- Position yourself at the bottom of the lift (watch the person in front of you to see the correct spot), with your skis parallel, about 22-30cm (9-12ins) apart.
- Put the straps of the ski poles around one wrist.
- Be ready to receive the button from the attendant. If there is no attendant at the lift, be ready to grab hold of the button with your free hand as it comes level with you.
- Hold the vertical bar firmly and put the button between your legs. Grip with your thighs.
- Flex your legs, balancing your weight over the balls of your feet and let the button push you along from behind. *Do not sit down on the button;* you must keep your knees and ankles flexed, taking your weight on your feet – not on your bottom.
- If the path of the lift is a little bumpy, just hold on to the bar tightly, and ride over the bumps by letting your ankles and knees bend to absorb the movement.
- As you near the end, gently pull down on the pole so that you can release the button from between your legs.

Master the snow plough turn by steering your foot in the direction of the turn. Then you can begin to link up your turns, enabling you to ski in both directions. This means that you can now control where you go across the slope.

29

● Let go – but not too soon; watch the people in front of you to see where they were when they let go.
● Step out to the side of the lift run, edging the inside of the skis so you do not slip backwards. Move away from the lift as quickly as you can.

Riding the T-bar

A T-bar is usually made for two people, so you must line up at the bottom, ready to receive the lift, with a partner. Position your skis parallel but rather closer together than you did on the button lift and hold your ski poles in your out-

T-bars are one of the commonest forms of uphill transport. They are easy to ride, but remember to step off quickly at the top.

side hand (*ie* the one on the outside of the T-bar). There is often a check board at the bottom of a lift to stop you sliding back; push the tails of your skis against it.
● Look behind you (over your inside shoulder) ready to take hold of the middle, vertical pole of the T-bar. Catch the bar and pull it down so that it rests just below your bottom.
● Flex your knees and ankles and allow the T-bar to push you forward. Do not sit down.

Stand with skis parallel and slightly apart; catch the button lift pole and hold it between your legs.

At the top release the button from between your legs, let go and step clear of the lift.

There is usually quite a sharp jerk as the T-bar starts off, so be prepared for this (that means flexing your knees and ankles).
● If the line of the lift includes a slight downhill section, as they often do, slow the skis down by edging the insides in a snow plough. Try to keep the bar in position all the time.
● At the top of the lift, decide with your partner which one of you will take the bar. If you are *not* going to take it, you must leave the lift *very slightly in advance* of your partner.
● As you approach the top, put your outside

Right: *To ride a T-bar, stand with a partner one each side of the bar. Hold your poles in the outside hand. Catch the bar with the inside hand. Pull it down so it rests just below your bottom. Do not sit down.*

Left: *When riding a drag lift you will encounter many bumps and hollows. Allow your legs to bend on the bumps and stretch in the hollows, so that your skis always remain in contact with the snow. Some drag lifts have downhill stretches.*

31

Skiing across the slope with the skis parallel is known as traversing. Maintain a straight line as you ski. Your skis should not slip sideways.

What if I fall off the lift?

Falling off a drag lift is another of those skiing certainties – everybody does it to begin with, so don't worry if it happens to you. The important thing to remember is to ask your instructor what he would like you to do in such an eventuality *before* getting on to the lift. It could be any one of the following:

● Take off skis and walk to the side of the slope. Wait for the instructor and class to come down and collect you.
● Take off your skis, walk down to the bottom of the lift and get on again (the class will wait for you at the top).
● If you fall off near the top, walk your skis up to the top of the slope. Only do this if you are very near the top; you will exhaust yourself otherwise!

Of course, it is important when you fall off to get out of the way of the oncoming skiers as soon as you can. Don't sit in the line of the lift to get your breath back; move to the edge first. And do not attempt to ski down the slope on your own at this stage – particularly if you have never skied it before.

How do I ski across the slope with my skis parallel?

Skiing with your **skis parallel** – almost all the time – should be your aim at the end of two weeks' skiing. There are various ways of achieving this aim. One is by learning the movements of the **basic swing.**

In its most refined form, a basic swing is a parallel turn – that is a turn in which the skis are parallel all the time. Before you can aspire to that however, it is necessary to break down the whole manoeuvre into a sequence of individual movements. As you refine each of these, you will reach a level of proficiency that enables you to combine all the movements in a smooth parallel turn.

To start a basic swing, you must first ski across the slope with your skis parallel – a manoeuvre that is traditionally known as a **traverse.** Skiing across the slope is essential for every skier, because there are few occasions when it is possible to ski directly down the mountain.

If you are to ski across the slope, however, you must learn more about **edge control,** for unless you exercise good edge control, your skis will merely slide sideways down the hill. In a traverse, the aim is to hold a specific line across the slope, without letting your skis slip sideways.

hand on the outer edge of the bar, and hold the central pole with your inside hand. Gently push yourself forwards and sideways off the bar, stepping away from it at an angle and letting go of it immediately.

● If you are the one left holding the pole, follow the same procedure as soon as your partner has stepped off, stepping out to the opposite side and letting the pole go at once. In both instances, make sure you (and your anorak) are well clear of the T-bar, before stepping off.
● If you have to cross the line of the lift to get to the skiing area, make sure you have plenty of time to do so without interfering with anybody coming up on the lift. Step across as quickly as possible.

What is the traverse position?

To achieve the correct traverse position, place your skis parallel across the slope about 20cm (8ins) apart with the upper edges set towards the hill (remember how to do this? – pressure on the little toe of the upper foot, big toe of the lower foot). Your lower ski should take the greater weight; think of it in terms of 60 per cent on the lower ski, 40 per cent on the upper ski. The top ski should be kept slightly in advance of the lower ski; the steeper the slope (or the further apart your skis), the further forward the top ski must be, in order to allow you to bend your knees evenly.

Adopt a mid-stance on your skis, with your knees and hips flexed forward. Your knees, hips and shoulders should be in direct line with the tips of the skis, so that you are facing straight down the direction in which you are travelling. This means your body will be inclined downhill along the line you are taking.

Use your poles to help you into this position. As you are pointing slightly downhill, you will need to support yourself on your poles to begin with. Take a very shallow line across the slope; then you will move very slowly, giving you lots of time to think about maintaining the correct position. Stop by moving your skis into a snow plough.

One of the most important features of skiing across the slope is to achieve good **edge control**. It is this that will enable you to hold a line across a slope. Try these exercises to help you improve your edge control:

● As you ski across the slope, sink down and touch your toes. Remember the important thing is not to deviate from the line.
● Ski across the slope, lifting and putting down the heel of the top ski.
● Ski across the slope hopping the heels of both skis up and down.

What do I do on steep slopes?

If you encounter a very steep part of the slope, where it is difficult to hold the line of the traverse and too steep to do a snow plough turn, you will want to find a way of moving down to a lower, less steep place. Think what would happen if you were in a traverse position and did not edge your skis; they would slide down the mountain, sideways. *Provided that you control this manoeuvre, – which is known as* **side-slipping** *– it can be extremely useful.*

Here is what you do. Position your skis in a traverse position across the fall line. Use your knees to flatten the skis, by rolling them gently outwards, or laterally down the hill. *Keep your upper body in the normal traverse position, with 60 per cent of your weight on the lower ski.*

As you flatten your skis, they will slip sideways, answering the pull of gravity. As they do so, maintain your balance, keeping that awareness of your weight on the lower ski, so that your body moves down the hill over your lower ski.

As you can see, side-slipping is certainly all about edge control and an exercise to help you with this is:

● Begin to traverse in a shallow line across the slope; flatten your skis with your knees as described above, so that you slip diagonally down the slope. Edge the skis again so that you go back into a traverse, then flatten them to side-slip some more.

Above: *If you feel that a slope is too steep to turn on, you can use a technique known as side slipping. Gently release your edges so that your skis are slightly flatter on the snow.*
Below: *Keep your weight over the lower ski.*

YOUR SECOND WEEK

The competent parallel skier has the whole mountain before him – all its different slopes, snow conditions, moguls, pistes, powder and perils. The skilled skier needs a wide range of techniques to adapt to every type of terrain he encounters.

It's only the beginning of your second week of learning to ski – and yet already you are a pretty competent skier! Certainly competent enough to go higher up the mountain to explore new slopes and ski areas. Think of it this way: the further you extend your ability and proficiency as a skier, the further you can extend up the mountain to find more demanding runs.

In order to go higher up the mountain, it will probably be necessary to take some other form of uphill transport, such as a cable car, a télécabine, a mountain railway or a long chair lift. The first three of these present no problem, for in all cases you merely step into them, carrying your skis. On some chair lifts you do not wear skis either; they travel up the hill with you, placed in a little pocket by the side of the chair. On most chair lifts, however, you will keep your skis on your feet.

Riding a chair lift is easy, particularly after the drag lifts. Stand with your skis parallel in the spot indicated by the attendant or at the bottom of the lift; look over your shoulder, ready to steady the edge of the seat with your hand as it approaches. Sit down quickly and keep the tips of your skis up to avoid any possibility of them sticking into the ground. Close the safety bar across the seat as quickly as you can.

Chair lifts may be for one, two or three people and will vary considerably in length according to the height of the slope. To get off at the top of the slope, release the bar, lean forward and push yourself off the chair, skiing away from the lift line.

What is the next move towards the basic swing?

The next move is to link the traverse movement which you have just mastered, with a snow plough, and back into a traverse. These movements will give you an **elementary basic swing** – elementary, because your skis are not yet parallel throughout the turn. The procedure will be to start off with your skis parallel in a traverse, to stem out the top ski into a snow plough, before bringing them back together in a traverse. You can see this illustrated in the left-hand column

Riding a chair lift is easy and usually gives you a wonderful view over the mountains. Stand ready, poles in one hand. Steady the seat with the other hand as it comes up to you. Sit down and pull the safety rail down in front of you.

opposite. Next to it is a **refined basic swing,** in which the stemming-out action has been reduced to such a degree, that in effect, it has been eliminated and the skis are moving parallel all the way through the turn. This is your aim, and if you go at it methodically – step-by-step – you will find it takes you very little time to achieve.

The basic swing – step one

We will take the traverse, snow plough glide and snow plough turn to be step one of the elementary basic swing. All these techniques you have long-since mastered. Now just put them together.

Start off the slope in a traverse – mid-stance on your skis. Brush out or lift the top ski with an up motion to take you up into a gliding snow plough. Stand high on your skis as they turn into the fall line. Apply pressure to what was the top ski, steering with your foot to do a snow plough turn. As you turn out of the fall line, try to slide in or lift the upper ski to put you back in a traverse. As you do this with speed, you will feel a skidding sensation – maybe for the first time.

Most people find the first stage of this – that is the traverse and the stem out of the top ski – quite easy to do. It is the second part of the turn that can cause problems, so we will work on this part. The aim now? To improve and refine the turning action from the fall line.

Step two

We will concentrate for the moment on an important aspect of turning that is fundamental to skiing. This is **skidding** your skis. Skidding, not slipping, is important in turning. Think about the gliding snow plough; as you do it, you can feel the skis skidding forwards and sideways against their inside edges. In a snow plough turn, when you apply weight to the turning ski, you can feel this ski skidding beneath you. The aim now is to skid both skis round the turn in a parallel fashion. This is done by bringing the skis together before or in the fall line, instead of turning out of the fall line in a snow plough turn and then bringing your skis together. If you bring the skis together quickly in the fall line, you will find they skid round together. This will only happen if they are steered against their edges. If you flatten the skis they will slip sideways.

Here are three ways of initiating a skid. In one and two, begin from a gliding plough in the fall line:

When you reach the last pylon on the chair lift, open the safety bar. This will leave your skis dangling free. Make sure the tips are up. As your skis touch the snow, push yourself off the seat forwards into a standing position. Lean forwards and ski down the ramp.

*This is the
elementary basic
swing. You begin
in a traverse, stem
out into a gliding
snow plough as you
turn out of the fall
line.*

*Steer skis round the
turn, then draw
them back together
into a traverse.*

1. Hop the inner ski parallel to the outer. The hopping action will create a skidding motion of the skis and you will feel them both sliding beneath you.
2. Lift the upper ski parallel to the outer ski. The lifting action combined with a down motion will cause a skidding effect.
3. Develop the skid by learning to shuffle. Begin in a steep traverse. Feel for the big toe of the

lower ski; press on it and displace the tail of the lower ski down the hill. (It's similar to a snow plough, except you are standing on the upper edges). Now feel for the little toe of the upper ski and press on it to bring the upper ski alongside. If you repeat this action in rapid succession, you will find that as long as you

*This is the refined
basic swing. In this
you eliminate the
stemming out
action and instead
turn your skis
parallel.*

*The edges are
changed by making
a strong up-motion
followed by a
strong steering
action. This is the
basic form of
parallel skiing.*

Skid your skis to help you turn. Shuffle the ski tails down the slope.

maintain the correct (uphill) edges of the skis whilst you quickly shuffle your heels round, you will feel the skis skidding freely beneath you. You need momentum and therefore a reasonable amount of speed to skid, which is why it is important to start off in a fairly steep traverse. In a shallow traverse you will not have sufficient momentum to enable your skis to skid round.

With these skidding exercises in your repertoire, try the whole turn again. Start off in a traverse, brush out and rise up into a gliding snow plough; *quickly* bring the skis together in the fall line and skid round the turn. Try individual turns to the left and right, and then try linking them together.

A useful way to help the skis skid round a turn is to look for quite a large hump in the snow. Aim for this in a traverse, stem out into a gliding snow plough as you approach the hump and draw the skis together sliding down the back of it. You will find the skis skid much more easily than they do on a flat surface.

It is only practice that will make you more competent at skidding your skis in a turn. You may find that your skis have a tendency to slide as you come out of a turn, making it difficult to hold the correct line. This happens if your skis are too flat; remember it is necessary to edge your skis in order to make them skid.

Step three

The concentration so far in trying to refine the basic swing, has been on skidding the skis out of the turn. This can be improved by applying a strong steering action, while skidding and this will improve the quality of the turn dramatically. As you know, good steering comes from the rotation of your feet and legs during the skidding phase of the turn. It is important now that you do not *lift* in the inner ski, but instead

steer it alongside the turning lower ski, until both skis are turning parallel, simultaneously, around the turn.

Start off in a plough in the fall line, now instead of lifting the skis together to skid them round the turn, feel for the outer edge of what will be the inner ski as you turn, by rolling your knee forwards and outwards in the direction of the turn. This will change the ski from its inner to its outer edge. Now with a down motion apply a strong steering action by turning both feet in the direction of the turn. The skis will come alongside one another and skid round the turn.

If you find this difficult in the fall line, try it by

Learning to skid your skis is an important part of turning. From a gliding snow plough, hop or lift the tail of one ski to bring it parallel to the other. This will give you the feel of skidding your skis.

Plough swing garlands will help you develop good rhythm in your turns.

Step four

The concern now is to ensure a good rhythm in the turn. Remember snow plough turn garlands, which involved the rhythmic action of coming up in the fall line and sinking down in the turn? You can do the same exercise with plough swings. **Plough swing garlands** can help to produce that all-important rhythm of *up* in the fall line and *down* in the turn. Plough swing garlands are just repeats of a plough swings in one direction.

Start in the fall line in a high gliding snow plough. Apply a down motion steering the inner

Start in a gliding snow plough in the fall line. Make a series of turns in the same direction. Practise this exercise in both directions for full effect.

They are called garlands because of the shape of the tracks left on the snow when doing continuous turns in one direction.

snow ploughing across the slope and drawing the top ski alongside.

So far, we have been concerned with refining the second part of the turn. This part of the turn is known as the **plough swing;** it is so called because it begins in a plough, after which the skis are brought together to swing round the turn.

Left: *Reducing the size of the stem and accompanying this with a strong steering action brings you closer to skiing parallel. Begin by reducing the stem by half.*

ski to create a steered, skidded turn. Come up, displacing the skis to move into a gliding snow plough turning into the fall line again. Repeat the action three or four times in both directions.

Plough swing garlands combine all the skills you have learnt, and particularly skidding and steering. The object now is to refine them sufficiently, so that you can come closer still to achieving a parallel basic swing. To do this, it is necessary to **reduce the stemming action** as you turn into the fall line.

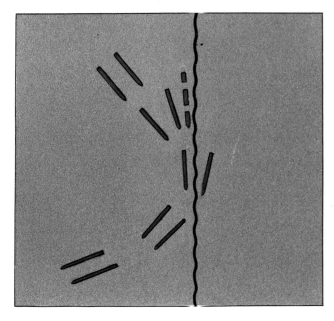

A parallel turn is brought about by the simultaneous changing of edges. To help in this process you need to take the weight off your skis. This is known as unweighting. Prepare for it by sinking down on the skis, flexing your hips and legs. Then extend your body upwards rapidly.

Step five

Reducing the stemming action and improving the steering action will enable you to keep your skis parallel throughout the turn. In other words, you have to steer and skid your skis *through the whole turn.* Thus we are beginning to concentrate on the first part of the turn – namely reducing the stem.

Begin by reducing the amount of stem taken from the traverse by about half. Traverse across the slope in a mid-stance, then with a strong up motion, stem out the top ski *half as much as usual and change edges.* Bring the skis together and steer strongly to skid them round the turn as quickly as possible. Try this in both directions.

In this exercise, the stem (or plough) is almost eliminated. By further reducing the amount of stem and accompanying this with a strong up motion, you will have achieved your first complete parallel basic swing. The key words now are **strong rhythm** and **unweighting.** A strong rhythmic action is something you have been aiming for in all your skiing exercises, right from your first day's skiing. Unweighting merely means the strong up motion you have been doing in many exercises; it momentarily takes the weight off your skis, so that you can change the edge. And it is that change of edge that will take your skis round in a new direction.

Let's run through the complete parallel basic swing again, as it is the fundamental basis of skiing parallel.

Step six

Start off in a good traverse, turn the skis towards the fall line using a vigorous extension, or upward motion of both legs, to facilitate the change from one set of edges to the other. Feel for the new set of edges and apply a down motion, combined with a strong steering action, to skid the skis around the turn and bring them into a new traverse. Remember to practise individual turns in both directions.

Can I use my poles to help me turn?

Your ski poles can certainly help you in turning, providing that you use them correctly. Properly used, your poles can do three things:
1. Help you to maintain the correct posture as you prepare for the turn and help you to time the beginning of the turn exactly.
2. Act as a trigger for the upward motion that allows you to change your edges and begin the strong steering action necessary to skid your skis.
3. Act as a turning pivot.

As you know, when you are skiing, your hands are held forward of the body, with the poles sloping diagonally backwards. When you plant a pole though, you have to bring it forward in order to place it close to the ski tip, about 10-15cm (4-6ins) out from the ski. It is essential that you swing the pole forward with a **wrist action,** not by using you whole arm.

Try this exercise to help you plant your pole effectively. Find a gentle slope and take up a straight running position, or schuss, with your body facing squarely down the hill. Sink down on your skis and as you do so, plant one pole beside the tip of one ski. As the pole is planted in the snow, come up on your skis in an unweighting action. Now sink down and plant the other

Use your pole to improve your turning. Plant the tips about 10-15cm (4-6ins) from the ski.

pole in the same way. Repeat the exercise, keeping a rhythmic action; say; "sink down . . . plant . . . up . . . sink down . . . plant . . . up".

The exercise leads on to using the pole plant as a trigger to hop up your skis (see hop parallels – page 45). Schuss down the fall line again, sink down, plant the pole and hop up your heels; sink down, plant the other pole and hop up your heels. The hop and up motion of your body is triggered by the pole plant. Bend your ankles, knees and upper body forward when planting the pole to give plenty of extension.

You can do a similar exercise in the traverse. Start off across the slope in a shallow traverse, sink down bending your ankles, knees and upper body forwards, plant the downhill pole and immediately bring your body up in an up-motion.

Another method of learning to ski parallel

As you may discover when you begin skiing, there is more than one route to progress towards, and finally achieve, parallel skiing. We have discussed the basic swing method, in which we learnt all the basic movements of an elementary basic swing; we have combined them and then set about refining them until we had achieved a parallel turn.

Some instructors or ski schools favour a different method, one from which you go straight from snow plough turns into parallel turns, without actually learning how to traverse or skid your skis. If you look at the diagrams on the opposite page, however, you will see that both these movements are actually incorporated within this turning method.

Accurate pole planting helps you to relax and position the body correctly for the turn.

The idea here is to link the snow plough turns with a strong, rhythmic up-and-down action accompanied by strong steering action with knees and feet. This is known as **plough wedeln.** By practising and refining it, you can eventually keep your skiis together through both turns. The progression is explained in the captions on the next page.

What do I do when I come to a bump directly in my way?

You just ski over it. It really is as simple as that! The terrain over which you ski, particularly as you become more and more proficient, will vary from flat, almost featureless piste, to steep moguls (see page 47), so it is important that the

Plough wedeln into parallel is an alternative to the basic swing. It can be a more direct method of learning to ski parallel. Begin by practising on fairly even terrain, making a series of turns.

Link up short, sharp snow plough turns, using strong leg movements and rhythm.

Work at building up a strong rhythmical action, steering quickly with alternate feet. Position your head over the steered ski in each turn.

Concentrate on steering the skis with a strong down-action. Accentuate the straightening of your legs, or up-motion, between your turns.

Keep your skis about 20cm (8ins) apart. Even when your skis are this close together, you should try to work your legs independently.

Ski slopes are seldom completely even, so you must learn how to ski over bumps and dips in the terrain. Let your legs act like the suspension of a car. As your ski tip hits a bump, bend your legs, by raising your knees towards your chest. Stretch your legs out into the hollow. Try to keep your head still and level all the time.

bumps you encounter in your path present no problem to you.

The technique now is to absorb the bump by compressing your lower legs. As your ski tips begin to rise up a bump, bend your legs by raising your knees towards your chest. Your knees should be most sharply bent when you are at the crest of the bump. Then, as you slide down the other side, slowly extend your legs; they should be almost straight in the hollows between bumps. Keep your head and upper body still; let your legs do the work. Someone watching only the top of your head as you ski down the slope should have no idea of the sort of terrain you are covering.

Bumps, far from being a nuisance or something to fear, can be extremely useful. Later you will learn how to use them to turn; and how they can make turning extremely easy!

Turning on a steep slope

It's quite right that you will find it arduous and tedious to try to do a clock turn on a steep slope, and yet you may well find yourself somewhere where you want to turn round to face the other way, with no room to ski round. So, do a **kick turn,** following the movements shown below. Important points to remember are to use your sticks behind you to give you support throughout the turn, but to position them so they do not get in your way or trip you up as you swing your ski round; and that the steeper the slope, the more you need to edge the uphill sides of the ski to stop you from sliding down.

A kick turn is useful for turning on steep slopes. Swing the lower ski round to point in the opposite direction. Stand on it to lift the other ski round.

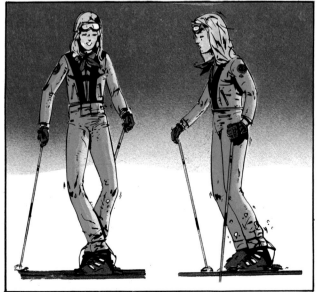

DEVELOP YOUR TECHNIQUE

As you progress, skiing higher on faster runs, you will need more advanced techniques. To turn fast you must keep your skis parallel. Once you can ski parallel you are no longer a beginner and you can think about attacking the more difficult, red runs.

You can do a parallel basic swing; you are now a **parallel skier.** Skiing parallel means just that, skiing with your skis parallel. However, there are many different sorts of parallel skiing techniques and there are equally, many levels of proficiency. The aim now, therefore, is to improve your parallel skiing and to learn to adapt it for the varied terrain you will encounter as you continue your skiing.

Should I keep working at my parallel basic swing?

You've come a long way in your skiing career – learning a lot of different movements, techniques and unfamiliar terms. It is more than possible that there are some aspects you will find particularly difficult – maybe you will find it hard to reduce the size of the stem or to make the correct strong steering action. Such things are not cause for worry – the basic technique will be established and there are all sorts of routes to take to improve your skiing. Rather than practise your weak points endlessly now – move on to something else, such as:

Hop parallels

The hop in a hop parallel is a means of changing the edges of the skis and is often taught as a useful exercise if you are having difficulty in reducing the stem in the parallel basic swing. Remember the traverse exercise, when you skied across the slope hopping up the heels of your skis? Now try this skiing straight down the fall line on a gentle slope, with your skis together. Sink down to prepare for the hop and plant your pole beside the tip of the ski. Use the pole plant to trigger the up motion and hop the tails of your skis.

Having done that a few times, repeat the exercise, but instead of just hopping up and down in the fall line, hop your heels out of the fall line and as you land sink down to steer the skis round the turn. The procedure then is – schuss down the fall line, sink down and plant the pole close to the tip of your ski, then hop your heels out the fall line the opposite side from the pole. As you land, sink down again steering into the turn with your knees and feet, letting your skis skid round into the traverse.

Right: *If you cannot eradicate the stemming action when turning, try hopping both skis across the fall line. But practise the hopping action first, by hopping up the tails of your skis as you schuss.*
Below: *Build up to a hop parallel turn by hopping out of the fall line before making a complete turn.*

Now try a complete **hop parallel turn:**

● Start in a *steep* traverse. Bring your downhill pole forward using a wrist action and sink down on your skis. Plant the pole and use it to trigger an up motion which will allow you to hop your heels so that the backs of your skis move just across the fall line. Immediately apply a strong down motion and steer your skis out of the fall line with your knees and feet.

Practise this turn to the left and right, then try linking turns. Vary them, making some long and sweeping, others shorter and tighter. Improve your technique by reducing and finally eliminating the hop.

A closer look at parallel turns

Good parallel turning is to do with good positioning and posture, accompanied by good balance on your skis. It can be broken down into three distinct phases:

1. Preparation – during which you look at the slope in front of you and determine *where* you are going to turn. Begin moving your wrist, ready to plant the pole and think of sinking down on your skis.
2. Anticipation – sink down and plant the pole. As you sink down, face your shoulders down the hill so that your body is ready to make the turn.
3. Extension – let the pole plant trigger the strong up motion which enables your skis to change edges before skidding round the turn.

It is impossible to achieve a good parallel turn unless each of these three phases are correctly executed, individually and in relation to one another, so it is worthwhile thinking of each of them carefully. The following exercise can help you with the preparation and anticipation phase: **Swing to the hill with a pole plant** Begin in a neutral or mid-stance in a traverse, sink down and prepare to plant the downhill pole ready for the turn, but as you sink apply a short, sharp checking movement by pressing your knees inwards to set the upper edges of the skis. The effect of this is to produce a short, exaggerated skid, which in effect, is a winding-up action for the extension that will follow. The check is an aggressive movement and by setting the edges this way, you provide a firm foundation for the turn.

Practise this movement by doing some garland exercises (just like those described on pages 28 and 39). Follow the checking of the skis with a short hop up the hill to take you into a steeper traverse. Then try some:

Short swing parallels These are powerful, edge-set turns, done one after another in a rhythmic movement. They are needed on a steep slope to control the speed of descent and they must be well executed. There is no time to recover between turns and you must keep them following on quickly from one another or you will soon be out of control, skiing flat out down the slope, before you know it! The finish of each turn is actually the platform from which to begin the next one.

Choose a steep slope, but not one that frightens you. Start in a snow plough and immediately

lift one ski over so that it is parallel to the other one. Straight away rebound off the edges and hop both skis across the fall line, using your poles as a support and a pivot. Land lightly on your toes and apply a strong steering action with a down motion. Keep your upper body and shoulders facing forward and squarely downhill (**angulation**). Repeat this action quickly and continuously. Keep your hands well forward all the time, angulate strongly.

What does angulate strongly mean?

Angulation is an important word in skiing. It means a forward bending at the hips to control the tendency of the upper body to follow the force of momentum in a certain direction, when the legs have turned to steer the skis in the other direction. To explain – as you ski, there is a force of momentum that is constantly driving your body. When you turn, that force will continue to drive your body in the direction it has just been travelling, *unless you make some adjustment to counteract it*. Think of a plough turn or a plough swing: when you sink down to make the turn, the upper body bends forward to compensate for the change in direction. That's angulation. On steep slopes, when a skier is travelling very fast, he must angulate strongly to maintain his equilibrium.

On steep terrain that has been made into piste (see page 69) and which is skied over continually, large bumps, known as moguls begin to appear. These are formed by skiers constantly turning, so that the snow is carved out and a bump is cut out of the snow.

Good parallel turns require careful positioning, together with good posture and balance.

How do I ski over moguls?

Very easily when you have mastered the technique. And you will enjoy it. Mogul skiing or mogul bashing is the ultimate skiing to some people. The steeper the slope and the bigger the bumps, the better they like it. You might be such a skier!

If you were to try to ski over the bumps turning with a fast up and down movement as you have been doing so far, the likelihood is that you would quite literally take-off – and provide onlookers with a spectacular display!

There are several skiing techniques for coping with moguls. Most have something in common, and are a form of **compression turn.** Ski schools in different countries all teach slightly different ways of executing these turns. In Austria, they use a technique called **wellen** (which means waves), in France it is known as **avalement** (which means swallowing up the bump) and in Italy it is **assorbamento** (which means absorbing the bump).

As always when skiing over bumpy terrain, try to keep your body as still as possible letting your legs do all the work. Let them retract on the highest point of the bump and stretch in the hollow after it. So – traverse towards the bump; as you approach it, retract or fold your legs beneath you so that you are in a compressed state; plant your pole on the top of the bump, directly downhill and *level with your feet* (not in front of them as before), and tilt your knees forward and in the direction of the new turn. Turn your feet to steer into the new direction and pivot round your pole. Your skis will turn easily, sliding round the back of the bump. As

Above: *You can use these short swing parallel turns to left and right where tight turns are needed to control your speed on steep terrain. Link your turns, using the finish of one turn as the platform for the next. Use your pole as a pivot. Land on your toes.*
Below: *Angulate by keeping your upper body and shoulders facing squarely down the hill, throughout a turn.*

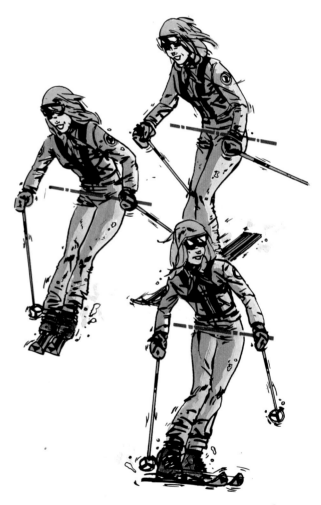

they slide down the side, extend your legs, still steering strongly with your feet. As you approach a mogul, say to yourself, "bend, turn, stretch".

Ski parallel – ski like the racers

Now you are able to ski parallel and turn round the moguls with compression turns, you might like to tackle some racing techniques. We said earlier that there were many methods of learning to ski – French, Austrian, Swiss and others – but when we come to ski racing, the differences are ironed out and techniques are very similar. Watch ski racers from different countries. Can you see much difference in the way they ski? In all cases, their upper bodies are held as still as possible, that is as still as the course will allow. The maximum power is coming from the movement of their legs, using very quick, strong steering actions. This should give you the feeling of carving a turn.

What is the first technique a racer learns?

A racer will always accelerate wherever he can in a race, working his skis to get the maximum speed from the terrain and the slope. To get that maximum speed, he must learn to skate – a technique which can be learnt and practised on the flat. In fact, it is a very useful way of propelling yourself along on flat ground.

Remember the herringbone method of going uphill – when you used the inside edge of one ski as a platform to project the other ski forward? (see page 19). That is similar action to **skating,** but now you must develop the action of pushing off from the inner edge of one ski onto the outside edge of the other ski so as to gain as much momentum as possible.

Start off on flat ground, with your skis together. Lift one ski and turn it outwards, as in a herringbone action. Feel for the inside edge of that ski and push away from it projecting the other ski forward. Glide forward on this ski for

Turning on moguls requires a technique known as the compression turn. Adopt a low stance in the fall line. Extend your legs as you turn, then as you transfer your weight to the outside ski, steer your skis round the corner, keeping them parallel.

This technique is known as the avalement in France. It means swallowing up the bump. As you approach the bump, begin to retract your knees, bringing them up towards your chest. Plant the downhill pole, wide of the body, close to the crest of the bump.

Skating is a useful method of propelling yourself along on skis. As a beginner you will find the skating action useful on the flat. Racers use skating as an important part of their technique. The top ski is stepped out laterally as high as possible. The lower ski is drawn alongside.

as long as possible. When you first try this exercise, keep both skis on their inside edges, but as you get the hang of it, try pushing off on to the outside edge of the gliding ski. As you reach the end of the glide, turn the ski on to its inside edge and propel the other ski forward in a glide. See how far you can propel yourself forward in each gliding move, keeping a rhythmic movement all the time. Use your poles to give you extra push.

As we have already said, the skating action can be used in downhill skiing to project more speed. It has its greatest application when used in a **skating turn** which is used mainly in giant slalom races. In a giant slalom race, the poles, or gates, are set further apart than they are in special slalom. If a skier skis down these gates using conventional parallel turns, he necessarily goes in quite wide arcs around the slalom poles. The aim of the event, however, is to race downhill as quickly as possible, so the racer therefore wants to stay as close to the poles as he can as this will save him time. A skating turn allows him to take a higher line to the gate, so that he can approach from a steeper, more direct angle,

rather than from the smooth curve of the previous turn.

Try a skating turn on an easy, smooth slope to begin with. Start in a steep traverse (it is necessary to have a fair amount of speed), step up the top ski applying pressure with the little toe of that foot so that you move onto the outside (top) edge of the ski. Immediately bring the lower ski up to it with a strong up motion. During this unweighted phase, change the edges with a knee movement and use a strong steering action of the knees and feet to take you round the turn.

What type of turn would be used in a special slalom race?

As we said, this wide long skating turn is not really suitable for special slalom where the gates are set closer together. A skating action is used but is disguised within the **step turn**. You will not find it easy to identify when watching slalom racers as it is often combined with other ski movements. However, the technique is often called **lateral projection**.

In special slalom the gates are close together, so racers use a skating step turn called lateral projection. Use the elementary basic swing technique, but instead of stemming out the ski, step it out quickly, with a strong up-motion.

The turn has a similar effect as the giant slalom skating turn, in that it puts you onto a higher more direct line for the next gate, but unlike the skating turn, it does not propel you forward with as much momentum.

A good way to develop the technique of this turn is to use an elementary basic swing, in which you would normally stem out the ski to make the turn. Instead of stemming it out, though, *step* it out quickly into the stem position, using a vigorous up motion. Immediately, draw the other ski alongside, then finish off the turn with a strong steering action. Try to keep close to the fall line as you step out and aim to

A relatively new and popular method of racing is the dual slalom. Skiers race side by side on identical and parallel courses.

keep reducing the amount of stem until it is eliminated. Now step out the ski parallel, change edges and instantly bring your other ski alongside, steering strongly to make the turn.

When you feel happy about this turn, try using it as you ski down a series of slalom poles. Remember that you want to step out into the new line as early as possible after turning through one gate and approaching the next one.

LEARN WITH SHORT SKIS

Methods of learning to ski vary from country to country.
In France and America particularly, short skis have been
used to help beginners. In France this is called Ski Evolutif.
In America it is called Graduated Length Method.

Ski Evolutif, or Graduated Length Method (GLM) is a system of teaching skiing, in which you begin on very short skis – 1 metre (just over 3ft) long – and graduate to longer skis as you improve. The system evolved as people involved with the teaching of skiing (in France and America in particular) realized that it would be much easier for a complete beginner to learn to ski on very short skis. This is because short skis are infinitely more manoeuvrable than long skis.

Many traditional, professional methods of learning to achieve parallel skiing are done away with in this system of teaching. Its exponents argue that traditional methods teach you how to snow plough and how to stem, only for these techniques to become redundant when you can ski parallel. Why not, therefore, teach the novice skier to ski with his skis parallel from the outset? As the short skis are so easy to man-oeuvre and turn, this is perfectly possible, and the skier learns techniques which are equally applicable to the longer skis he will ultimately use. In fact, it is quite possible that some of the basic techniques, such as a snow plough, will be taught at a later stage; they are just not included as part of the basic learning pattern.

If you were to take a course in Ski Evolutif or GLM, you would find there was far less formal-ity – verbal instruction and explanation – than is normal in a traditional ski school. Instead the teaching philosophy draws heavily on the fun aspect of learning to ski – and fair enough, for if it's not fun, what is the point of it all? The instructor has the class playing games that involve the use of some particular technique, so that they just 'come across it', rather than being actively instructed to do it.

The great exponent of the Ski Evolutif method in France was Robert Blanc, and he set up a teaching school in the resort of Les Arcs. He described it as an aggressive method of skiing in which the pupil, because he feels more secure on his skis, does not act in the defensive manner so often seen when being taught on traditional, longer skis.

It is not possible in this book to follow the comprehensive progress of learning through a Ski Evolutif system, in the same way as we have followed the more traditional teaching method. Many of the techniques are the same anyway, so we have outlined some of the principal activities in the pictures and descriptions overleaf.

Ski familiarization Even though the skis are so much easier to handle, you must still become accustomed to having them on your feet. Try jumping up the tips, then the heels; stepping sideways and forwards; sliding backwards and forwards; lifting up the entire ski and putting it down level; turning round by jumping in the air and moving the skis a quarter of a circle. You will not use ski poles for some time in this method; so hold your arms out at shoulder level to help you maintain your balance.

Side-stepping Another similar technique is that used to climb up a slope. Take small steps uphill, with your skis positioned across the fall line in just the same way as described on page 19. Remember to let your upper body bend slightly downhill to give a banana, or crescent-moon shape over the downhill ski. Going uphill using the herringbone method is much easier on short skis, and apart from skating, will be almost the only time your skis are not parallel.

Skating As you have no ski poles to help propel you along, you will find the easiest way to move around on flat ground is to skate. The technique is the same as that described on page 50.

Play Playing games in groups is an integral and important aspect of this system of teaching. Perhaps you will ski along holding hands, or play leapfrog on skis (being careful!) or take part in relay races following each other over a prepared course. There are lots of games to play with balloons – try skiing along holding them between your legs, or throwing them to one another as you ski down a gentle slope.

Traversing The traverse position is just the same as that used on longer skis. You may not know you are being taught how to traverse, though – your instructor will just set you skiing across the slope. Try executing slight checks as you go, by using a twisting action of the knees to swivel the skis up hill and to edge them. Remember – your shoulders should not move. Relax your skis and continue in a traverse.

Schussing down fall line *Learning to ski straight downhill is easy on short skis and best learned in groups— by playing trains. Slide down the hill in a group holding on to the person in front. Another way is to walk up the slope together holding hands, turn around and ski down in a line across the mountain, still holding hands.*

Stepping out of the fall line
Remember skating – when you pushed off the inside edge of one ski onto the outer edge of the other ski to propel you forward or change direction? Use this technique now to slow you up when schussing down the fall line. As you schuss down the slope, step out onto the top edge of one ski and *quickly* bring the other ski alongside. It's that old friend – little toe, then big toe. If you keep repeating this action, you will stop as your skis will soon be facing uphill.

Jumping and skidding
Exercises involving jumping and skidding will give you the initial feeling of a skidded turn. Begin by schussing down the fall line and hopping up the heels of your skis. Then schuss down the fall line and hop the heels outwards. Absorb the landing by sinking down on your skis and swivelling your hips to change the direction. Your skis will automatically skid round. Practise hopping from side to side out of the fall line, keeping your weight on the lower ski and edging the uphill edges as you come into the turn. This is known as **twisting** down the fall line.

Extension Throughout this book we have used the terms **high-stance**, **mid-stance** and **low-stance** to describe the posture you must adopt at various times. When you are hopping the skis, you are in a high, or extended, stance.

Skidding parallels These evolve quite easily from your jumping and skidding exercises. Ski across the slope in a traverse, hop up the tails of the skis, changing the edges to change the direction. As the skis are so short, very little effort is needed to turn them. Try to eliminate the hop by making it smaller until you are really just swivelling and turning the skis using a steering action with your feet and knees.

Pole planting As you gain proficiency on short skis you will naturally move on to the next length, and you will also begin to use the ski poles actively. All the techniques you have learnt remain the same whatever length ski you use.

CROSS-COUNTRY SKIING

In Scandinavia men have been using skis for winter transport for thousands of years. Today cross-country skiing, which is like walking on skis, is almost as popular as downhill or Alpine skiing. Many resorts have special tracks for the cross-country skier.

Modern skiing is divided into two major disciplines – **Alpine** or **downhill,** and **Nordic.** So far we have been discussing the techniques and equipment used in Alpine skiing, and yet Nordic skiing was in existence long before the concept of downhill skiing emerged, less than a hundred years ago.

Skiing, as a means of travelling over ice and snow, is an extremely ancient activity. The oldest ski so far discovered was found in a Swedish peat bog and has been dated as being nearly five thousand years old. Clearly, prehistoric man found he could move across the snowy ground more easily if he attached long, flat boards of wood to his feet. Ever since that time, men have been skiing in order to go from place to place in the winter.

It is from these practical roots, that modern cross-country skiing, or ski-touring, has developed, although it is now widely practised as a sport and relaxation, rather than as a form of transport. Cross-country skiing is not the fast, dynamic, aggressive sport that downhill skiing is. Instead, it is an infinitely more tranquil activity, more like simply walking along on skis

An important event in competitive Nordic skiing and in the Winter Olympics is the biathlon. This is a long distance race over 10km (6 miles), which includes a test of target shooting. The Russians have proved the most successful in recent years.

- a means, in fact, of going for a winter walk.

Cross-country skiing is no longer confined to the northern countries of its origin. Over the last ten years it has emerged as a sport that offers a real alternative to downhill skiing, particularly in the Alps and North America, as well as in Australia and New Zealand. Most major ski resorts now have marked and graded cross-country trails and circuits and many, many people – of all ages – are beginning to find that it is a sport they can really enjoy. It is interesting to note, though, that Nordic and Alpine techniques are beginning to draw closer together, as Nordic skiers develop similar methods of handling the downhill aspects of cross-country skiing.

Modern ski techniques have evolved from traditional methods of the past. Here a Scandinavian single pole technique is demonstrated.

The basic techniques of cross-country skiing

As in all aspects of skiing, the first thing to do is to get the feel of the skis. In cross-country skiing, this can lead quickly into the principal movement – **the two-phase diagonal stride.** This is the action that enables the skier to move, seemingly without effort, with long, easy, gliding strides.

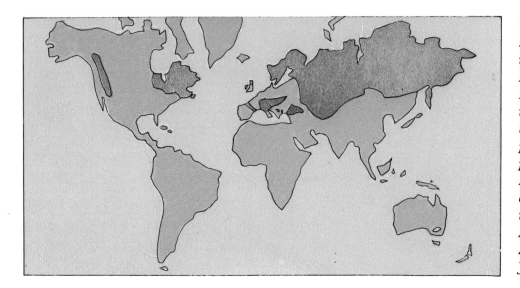

Today cross-country skiing is practised in Northern Europe and Russia, as well as many other parts of the world. It is popular in many parts of North America and attracting more and more people in Australia, New Zealand and Japan.

To begin with, just shuffle your feet forward alternately on a flat area of ground. Try to achieve, and *feel*, a short gliding action of your ski each time you move one or other forward. Use your arms to balance you; do not attempt to use your poles to push you along at this stage.

Try turning round, just stepping around the tips and heels, as in the clock turn (see page 18).

Now map out for yourself a small circuit on a flat area and ski round it, aiming to improve your gliding and turning. Imagine an exaggerated walking action in which you stride out strongly, swinging your arms freely. Don't lift the skis. Try to make the leading ski glide for as long as possible before bringing the other one forward. Think of **kicking** off the rear ski by applying a downward pressure.

Your arm action is very important in helping you to maintain a rhythm as you ski. It needs to be vigorous to co-ordinate the striding action. Be aware of really swinging your arms – up to chin level in front and high behind you, keeping your arms relatively straight as you swing them.

We have led into this two-phase diagonal stride by suggesting that you learn to shuffle your skis to get them to glide forward, because as a beginner, you will find it impossible to perform an efficient diagonal stride from a stationary position. It is best developed when in full stride, bearing in mind the following key factors:

- The kick forward onto a gliding ski is the trigger to the whole two-phase movement. Your body should be leaning forward, your hips and knees slightly bent, with your weight over the kicking foot.
- Kick downwards and backwards with a sharp and vigorous action. Swinging your arm forward and upwards, also vigorously, will help to increase the downwards force over your foot. Stretch your body trunk forwards.
- As you kick down, transfer your weight on to the gliding ski, feeling your weight balanced over the ball of your foot. This is the second – or resting – phase of the movement.

The two-phase diagonal stride is the first movement a cross-country skier learns. It is so called because the opposite arm and leg work together. The skier moves with long, easy gliding strides.

Learn about weight

Where you place your weight over your skis will greatly influence the performance and quality of your cross-country skiing just as it does in Alpine skiing. Knowing how – or when – to transfer your weight from one ski to another can help you to develop and improve the diagonal stride. The various stride patterns you will learn are based on when you transfer the weight, combined with when you plant the pole.

Right: *The exact moment at which you transfer your weight from one foot to another is an important part of cross-country skiing.*
Right: *To change direction, put weight on the outside ski. Bend inside knee and turn ski. Use outside ski and poles to push off in new direction.*
Below: *This is the three phase alternate stride. The skier gives two pushes with her poles for every three strides. The black lines below indicate the ski taking the skier's weight. The circles show the point of the pole plant.*

Transfer your weight onto your gliding ski as you kick your heel down after the forward push. This allows you to really push the ski forward. Do not be tempted to shift the weight too early; if you do, the glide will be considerably shortened. To transfer the weight effectively, it is necessary to loosen the hips and to bend the knees and ankles, as you prepare to kick down.

Learning to skate on the skis can help you with transferring your weight, as in skating, it is a vigorous and definite movement. You have to throw your weight onto the gliding ski or you will make little forward progress. Skating in this way is very similar to skating in Alpine skiing (see page 50). Place one ski at a V-angle to the other and push off it onto the other ski. Shift your weight immediately, throwing your body forward and slightly in the direction of the leading ski. Use your poles to give you more propulsion.

When you feel you have developed a reasonably competent diagonal stride, you can begin to use the poles to help push yourself further forward. The way in which you use your poles can

have a great effect on the rhythm of your stride, the position of your body on the skis and the speed at which you travel.

Plant the pole level with your leading foot, using a downward and backward drive. Initially you pull on the pole (**pole pull**) changing to a push as you drive your arm backwards (**pole push**). The pole should always be angled backwards – the basket should *never* come in front of your hand. If it does, it will cause a braking, rather than a propelling action. Relax your grip after the drive then bring the pole forward again, swinging your arm past your hip. Never try to lift it – just swing it.

The diagonal stride, the transference of weight and the use of your poles can be used to change the direction of travel. Begin with your skis parallel and then follow the movement shown in the diagram opposite. The caption gives further instructions.

Striding patterns

When you have mastered the basic diagonal stride, you can begin experimenting with the

Above: *You can use your poles to propel you along. This is the double pole push. Plant your poles together just in front of your feet. Pull on them, then push down.*
Right: *Use the skating step to accelerate on the flat.*

tempo – that is the number of strides you take per minute – and the **stride length** – that is how far you travel with each stride. Try making faster movements, increasing the tempo and reducing the length of stride. Then try increasing the stride length and reducing the tempo.

Occasionally try using your poles simultaneously in a **double pole push** as shown above. In this, you keep your skis together – there is no striding – and use a vigorous arm movement to propel your skis along. You can use this to keep you moving along on the flat whilst giving your

This is the four phase alternate stride. In this the skier gives only two pushes with the poles for every four strides she makes. This and a three phase alternate stride, can be used on level ground to give your arms and back a rest.

To move uphill you can use the diagonal stride, but make the sliding step forward shorter as the slope gets steeper.

legs a rest, or to gain more speed on gradual down gradients. It does require considerable bending of the body from the waist and a strong arm action.

As you increase your speed and fluency, you will need to develop a rhythm of muscle tension and relaxation or you will find yourself tiring quickly. Learning, and putting into effect, variations in striding patterns – such as the three or four phase patterns – will help you. Not only is the striding action less vigorous, but the pole is not planted at every stride, as you can see. This gives your arms and your back a rest.

You can use the bumps and hollows you encounter on the tracks around which you ski to help you to accelerate. Time your strides so that you can push off from just below the crest of the bump.

Uphill technique

Obviously when touring you will need to travel uphill – you can't keep sliding gently downhill for ever! Striding uphill is not as difficult as it sounds. It requires a more active and aggressive approach. Imagine you were on a cross-country run and you came across a bank. What would you do? Without thinking, you would shorten your stride, shift your centre of gravity slightly forward and use a much more aggressive arm action as you run up the incline. This is exactly what you do on skis; your movements must be well co-ordinated and more powerful than usual.

Kicking off the bumps

Undulating and bumpy terrain is as much a feature of ski touring as it is of Alpine skiing, and both skiers need to ski smoothly over bumps and through hollows. Use the bump to your advantage to help you accelerate. Allow your skis to ride over it gently, then kick off the back side of the bump – just as an athlete springs off his blocks. As you become more confident, you can push off the bump with a double pole action. This is particularly useful if you need the speed to carry you to the crest of the next bump. It is the timing of your strides that is important in this action: you may have to lengthen or shorten your stride so as to ensure you are correctly positioned to push off the back of the bump.

Equipment

Cross-country ski equipment differs greatly from that used by sophisticated Alpine skiers; it is infinitely more simple.

The skis Touring skis are generally longer and narrower than their Alpine counterparts. As a beginner you will be faced with a choice of

length, type of flex and whether to pick a waxable or waxless type. The combination of your weight, height and snow conditions will determine the length and degree of flex you should select, but generally a novice skier should opt for a fairly soft ski. You can test the stiffness of a pair of skis by placing them back to back and pressing them together. A good pair of racing skis would be almost impossible to push together; a soft pair you could press together with the pressure of one or two fingers. As a beginner and a tourist, it is best to go for a ski that needs very little maintenance of the sole – that is, a waxless type. Leave the sophisticated waxable variety to the experts and the racers.

Cross-country skiers can race in vast numbers (one race in Sweden has 10,000 competitors) or they can ski alone in the winter countryside.

Bindings These comprise a simple hinge design to hold the front of the boot, with a small heel-locating plate to stop the boot from slipping sideways and to prevent the snow from sticking under the sole (your heel is not held firmly on the ski in the way it is with Alpine skis). A variety of types exist, but they are all the same in principle: that is, they are designed merely to connect the boot to the ski. The differences occur according to whether they are meant for touring or racing.

Modern waxless skis have many different patterns and sole surfaces. All provide grip.

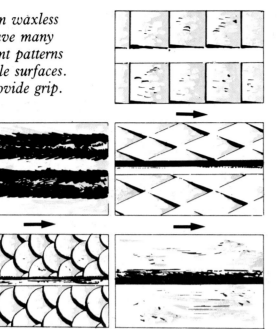

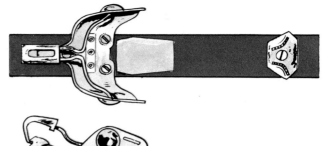

Poles These should have a sturdy, durable shaft, strong steel tips and round supporting baskets (for soft snow). The grips should feel comfortable in your hand and the wrist straps should be adjustable. You can establish whether they are the right length by standing up straight on a pair of skis and putting the tip of a pole on the top surface of the ski, just behind the heel. If the pole fits snugly under your armpit – without you having to raise your arm – it is the right height. Remember that poles for cross-country touring should be designed to take a bashing; durability is likely to have been the most important criterion in their manufacture.

Boots Good quality, comfortable and well-fitting boots are essential, for nothing will ruin your enjoyment of ski touring more quickly than cold, wet and sore feet. They are much lighter than Alpine skiing boots and give little support to your ankles. They should be flexible in the forward plane, like a soft shoe, but laterally, they must be stiff. The uppers need to be durable and waterproof while allowing your feet to breathe and keeping them warm. Boots should fit snugly with room to move the toes for warmth and when flexed forward they should not cause pain across the instep. Avoid cheap, flimsy boots which will impede immediate transference of movement. Those made of quality leather are excellent, but very expensive. Most people choose one of the many synthetic types that are available now. These are waterproof, yet allow moisture to pass out. You will find that boots are classified as general touring, light touring and racing boots.

Clothing As always, it is important that the

Above: *Bindings on touring skis are designed to hold only the toe of the boot. They have a hinge which allows the foot to swing upwards. On the heel there is a locating plate.*
Right: *Boots should flex forwards but not sideways.*

clothes you wear will keep you warm and dry in the circumstances in which you are skiing. Thus, someone touring gently round low-level tracks will require different clothes from the ski mountaineer. Recreational cross-country skiers generally wear a specially-designed all-in-one suit or special knee-length breeches with thick, long socks. Top garments in this instance should be comfortable, not restricting arm movement in any way. They should be waterproof, but should allow for a free outward passage of air and moisture.

Under-garments would be similar to those worn for Alpine skiing, as would a hat and gloves. Don't forget to wear sunglasses or goggles – the reflection and glare from the snow are very strong.

Waxing skis

The modern trend among recreational ski tourers is to use waxless skis. There are many different patterns available, as shown in the diagram, and such skis are easy to maintain. Most beginners and intermediates, or those with only a limited amount of time to spend skiing each year, generally do not want to be bothered – nor spend the necessary time – to prepare and wax skis – even when they have acquired the necessary skill and knowledge to use the wax cor-

rectly. Waxing skis is an exacting art. Done properly, it allows a skier to obtain the maximum performance from his skis, which is why racers and experts always use waxable skis. The waxes they use fall into two basic categories – **grip waxes** and **speed waxes.** The former are used by ski tourers; the latter mainly by the racers.

Ski mountaineering

Nordic skiing must be skiing in its purest form, for it encompasses all aspects of skiing. But by far the most serious and demanding aspect of cross-country skiing is ski mountaineering. Tak-

Ski mountaineering expeditions can be exciting adventures, but they are not for beginners.

ing on the high mountain ranges is a very different story from learning ski touring techniques on prepared trails, around the local villages. Ski mountaineering calls for judgement (which could affect life and death), knowledge and the right equipment. The ski mountaineer has to be highly competent and his knowledge has to cover such areas as meteorology, rock climbing, navigation, survival technique and mountain safety. Ski mountaineering is not for beginners.

IN THE MOUNTAINS

High mountains should command the respect of every skier. They can be dangerous, although great efforts are made to make ski areas as safe as possible. Everyone should know what to expect in mountain conditions and what to do in an emergency.

To ski you must go to the mountains. But for most of us the mountains are an alien environment – one in which the extremes of temperature and weather conditions, high altitude and lack of civilization can become hazards to the unwary or the unprepared. Mountains can be dangerous; this is a fact that many people either do not always realize or take into account.

Many of the mountain hazards are less extreme for the skier than for those who follow more lonely mountain pursuits, such as climbing. Cable car stations, mountain restaurants, trained ski patrols and the sheer number of people on the ski slopes have made them artificially safe places to be. The various pistes and lift systems act as the skier's road and motorway links for mountain travel, guided by a piste map, like the one on page 69.

The effects of altitude

As you go higher up a mountain, the temperature drops, the winds become stronger and yet you are more likely to be burnt by the sun. The sun's rays are stronger (but not warmer) at the top of the mountain where there are fewer dust particles in the air, which would otherwise filter out the ultra violet rays. It is ultra-violet rays that cause sunburn. The snow reflects the rays with great intensity, particularly late in the season, when the sun is stronger.

If you are going to ski high in the mountains, you must protect yourself against such conditions. Make sure you have enough warm clothes and protect your face (lips particularly) with sun cream and lip salve. If you have a fair, sensitive skin, use a sun cream that has a high filtering factor – five or six. Remember always to take your sun glasses or goggles with you, to protect you from the glare.

Most European resorts use a colour code to classify the runs, so that you can see at a glance which are the easier ones and which are the more difficult. Nursery slopes or very easy runs are generally coloured **green;** those coloured **blue** are a little more difficult – say for skiers who can snow plough, turn and traverse. **Red** runs are much more difficult and are generally considered suitable for intermediate to good skiers. **Black** slopes are for advanced skiers only; they are very difficult and can be very dangerous in icy conditions.

Weather conditions

Probably the worst weather you can encounter in the mountains is fog. When it descends over the mountain, it is known as a **white-out** and in these conditions you are not able to see the difference between the snow and the sky. There is nothing worse than skiing on a run you do not know in a white-out. If you find yourself in a fog follow the markers on the piste. If you are in a group, stretch out to look for the markers, but keep in contact with each other, and make sure everyone is present each time you make a move down the mountain. This is a prime example of why it is most unadvisable to ski alone.

The snow conditions you can expect to encounter are described below, but remember any particular run will not always have the same snow conditions, and indeed these can vary at different times of day, according to the weather and the aspect of the slope. South-facing slopes, which were lovely to ski on in the morning, may have soft, mushy snow conditions later in the day when the sun has been shining on them for several hours. North-facing slopes tend to be cold all the day long and could be very icy too.

Another factor that can effect snow conditions is wind. It can shape the surface leaving a wave-like crust across it; it can blow away the surface after a snow fall or melt the top layer of snow which later turns to ice. Be aware of the weather conditions, so that you are ready to make allowances for the changes in ski conditions they may cause.

Piste signs

Learn to recognize and understand the various signs you encounter on the piste. Many are similar to international road signs. The most important sign to recognize is the one that tells you that a particular run is closed. This will be stated in the language of the country in which you are skiing, so find out what it is, and never ignore a closed sign on a piste.

Above: *Warning signs*. Below: *The Matterhorn*.

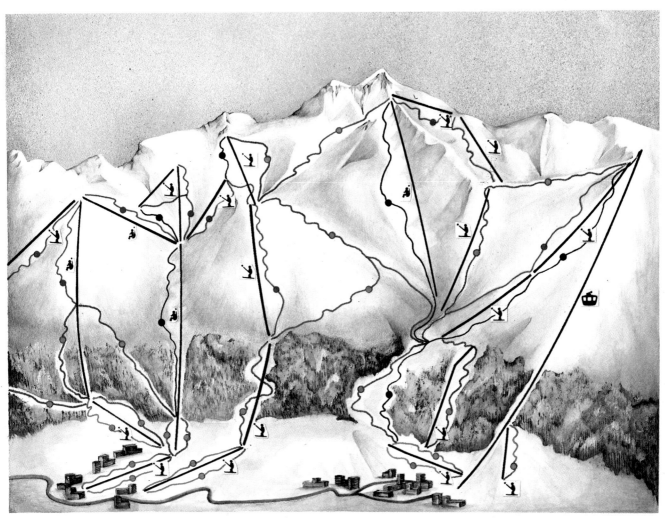

Snow conditions

These are the principal variations in snow conditions that you may encounter.

Piste A pathway or route of compressed snow, usually well marked and prepared by special piste machines.

Powder A surface of very small ice crystals that blow about like dust, usually found after a fresh fall of snow.

Wet heavy snow (known also as porridge or mashed potato). It is damp to the touch and it sticks to boots. It is very difficult to ski in such conditions.

Crust There are two types – that caused by the sun melting the surface snow, after which it has refrozen, leaving a surface that is shiny and roughened; or that caused by the wind blowing falling snow into lee drifts and compacting it. In this instance, the surface has a dull, satin appearance. Generally this is difficult, but not dangerous for the skier. The sun crust on the other hand, will often not carry the skier's weight and is dangerous.

Spring or corn snow Very large crystals which are formed by the repeated melting and freezing of the snow cover.

This is an imaginary piste map, similar to those given away free at most resorts. A piste map tells you about a resort's runs and facilities. It can also help you see where to go in an emergency.

Ice Smooth and solid glass-like surface caused by the rapid freezing of a very wet snow.

Tramlines Old ski tracks which have frozen solid. They are dangerous if you get your skis wedged in them – avoid this by skiing over them at right angles.

Thin snow Recognizable by the grass, roots or rocks showing through the surface. Best avoided as objects under the surface can catch on the soles of the skis.

Most of your skiing will be done on the piste; indeed all of it should be, unless an instructor takes you off it for any reason. Most resorts have a high standard of piste maintenance. Piste machines will run over the surface at regular intervals to keep the snow smooth, and experienced skiers, known as the ski patrol, check the pistes during the day to make sure everything is all right. They will also ski down the pistes last thing in the afternoon, just before the pistes are closed, to make sure no one is still on them.

If there is an accident follow the rules carefully.

Accident procedure

All skiers must know what to do in the event of an accident, particularly those in which a skier appears to be badly hurt.

- Prevent further accidents by warning others. Place a pair of skis, crossed in the snow, well above the skier.
- If the victim is near the brow of a hill on a narrow piste, he should be moved out of the way of oncoming skiers if at all possible. If it is not possible to move him, position someone further up the piste to stop skiers.
- Send two people down the hill (a proficient skier or a ski instructor could go on their own) to inform the ski patrol of the accident. Give them *precise details* of the location of the accident, either by marking it on a piste map if you can, or by giving the number of any ski lift or pylon that is near by.
- Keep the injured person warm and still until the ski patrol arrive. If you are qualified to give first aid and it would be beneficial, do so.

The ski patrol will take the injured person down the mountain. From there he will be taken to an X-ray unit or nearby hospital. When he has received the necessary treatment, he will be taken back to his hotel, injuries permitting.

Avalanches

Avalanches may occur after a really heavy snow fall, when the new snow does not hold onto the old snow underneath straight away. They may occur when a storm blows snow into the air. If the wind drops, the snow falls suddenly, causing a pressure wave that can travel at up to 300kph (185mph). Or they may occur in the spring when the snow begins to melt and loses its hold on the ground underneath.

Normally, you will not be skiing in potential avalanche areas, but if for any reason you are — there are precautions you can take.

- Wear an avalanche cord. This is like a streamer that you throw out over the snow to mark your position.

There are several kinds of avalanche. Dry snow avalanches (1) create blasts of air. Slab avalanches (2) are broken snow crust. A wet snow avalanche can be on an even slope (3) or in a valley (4).

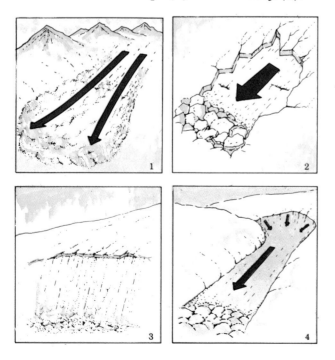

- Make all the members of the group spread out.
- Cross any potential danger spots as high up and as quickly as you can, in single file.
- Take ski sticks off your wrists and safety straps off your ankles. If the conditions are really bad, take off your skis and walk.

The skiway code

By observing the skiway code, you can do much to ensure you do not cause an accident. Just like the highway code – these rules are made for the safety of skiers.
- The slower skier always has right of way.

- When overtaking slower skiers, pass uphill of them, giving them as wide a berth as possible.
- Do not attempt dare-devil feats of skiing that are beyond your ability; you will be a nuisance and a danger to others. Ski within the limits of your skill.
- Learning and observing the piste signs, and never skiing alone are aspects of the ski-way code that you should never forget.

Piste machines are used in modern ski resorts to prepare the marked runs (pistes). Runs are graded according to how difficult they are.

WHERE TO GO FROM HERE

As a skilful skier you will find new resorts, conditions and contests to challenge you. Maybe the fun of freestyle, the sensation of off-piste skiing, or the world of racing are where your ambitions lie.

The answer to this problem is probably into some sort of competitive skiing, for modern developments in skiing and ski techniques mean that there is a form of competition to suit every skier.

Nordic skiing evolved from its practical background into a popular sport as new, better equipment began to be developed. Nowadays, the sport of Nordic skiing is divided into **ski-jumping, cross-country, sprinting** and **biathlon.**

Ski-jumping is as it sounds – a jump made on skis. Competitors ski down a man-made chute situated high on a mountain, and at the bottom of it, they launch themselves into the air to land some considerable distance down the hillside. In a competition, they are judged on style and landing as well as the length of the jump.

Cross-country is long distance racing around a prepared course that may be anything from 5-50 kilometers (3-30 miles) long. Sprinting is a race over a much shorter distance, which means the skiers can afford to sprint rather than having to pace themselves over a longer route. The biathlon involves a long distance race over 10 kilometers (6 miles) as well as a test of target shooting proficiency.

Alpine or downhill skiing did not really become an important sport until early in this century, but it did not take long to establish a stronghold and become fantastically popular. Competitions on skis soon began, and were influenced particularly by an Englishman, called Sir Arnold Lunn, who invented slalom racing. The first slalom competitions were held at Murren in Switzerland in 1922.

As skiing techniques have advanced with the development and constant refining of skis and equipment, so various competitive skiing events have evolved in the Alpine discipline. Best known among these are **special slalom, giant slalom** and **downhill.**

A slalom race involves racers skiing down a prepared, marked course along which poles or gates are positioned. The skiers have to choose the fastest path through these gates and the course will have been designed to allow them to adopt a flowing rhythm, whilst thoroughly testing their ability. In special slalom the gates are positioned very close to one another. In a men's race, there are generally between 50 and 70 gates; this number is reduced to between 40 and 60 for women. In giant slalom racing, the course is set over a greater distance and the gates are

A magnificent inversion, one of many tricks that are part of freestyle skiing.

spaced further apart. Competitors therefore can ski much faster as they can take a straighter line through the gates.

Downhill is probably the most exciting competition of all, at least for the spectator. In this the course is considerably straighter than in the slalom races. The gates mark the edges of the piste rather than acting as turning obstacles. Skiers hurtle down the mountain at up to 130kph (80mph), adopting a position on their skis known as **the egg.** This is a low crouch, in which their body is bent into an oval or egg shape. Such a position helps to reduce wind resistance (which makes them go faster) and also helps to keep them in close contact with the ground. When skiing really fast, the slightest bump in the terrain will cause the skis to take off into the air – and that means vital hundredths of a second lost. The skier needs to react very quickly, adjusting his **dynamic posture** for all changes in the terrain, returning to the egg position whenever he can.

Throughout the winter, slalom and downhill races are held for international skiers and there are many resorts famous for racing. Downhill courses must conform to the Federation Internationale de Ski regulations, which state for example, that all dangerous obstacles must be cleared from the course and that the minimum course width through trees or forest areas should be 30 metres (100ft). They also stipulate that all competitors must wear crash helmets; a tumble taken at the speed necessary for success in such competitions can mean extremely serious injury to a skier. St Anton, Wengen, Kitzbuhl and St Moritz are often the venue of the classic downhill races.

The youngest of all Alpine ski disciplines and one which is only just beginning to produce international competitions, is **freestyle.** This is an entirely new form of self-expression on skis. It is individually creative and is not dominated or even restricted by the usual ski techniques. In effect, freestyle skiers are similar to acrobats or dancers. The freestyle movement was begun by extrovert skiers in the United States of America who were looking for new ways to vary the routines of skiing. Now it has spread far and wide, and skiers in Britain and Europe are turning to it more and more.

Freestyle skiing has three main activities:

- **Mogul skiing** A skier skis down a mogul field in the most exciting way possible. No series of simple compression turns for him; instead he tries to devise stunts to take him straight over the moguls. The most fantastic and extreme stunts win the most points.
- **Aerials** These are really ski acrobatics. Skiers will be seen turning somersaults, spinning, jumping – generally executing all sorts of breathtaking movements. Aerials are divided into **inversions, spins** and **uprights.**
- **Ballet** This is the gentlest and most aesthetic of the activities and is usually performed on gentle slopes. Skiers literally dance on their skis, executing figures, some of which are similar to those of ice skating.

Steve McKinney, the first man to achieve 200kph (111mph) on skis, at Portillo, Chile.

Off-piste skiing

To ski off-piste in good snow conditions is the ultimate pleasure for a skier. It is a freedom you cannot discribe. Skiing virgin snow is almost intoxicating, giving you a wonderful sense of well-being.

If you can ski parallel with good posture and pole plant, you can ski in deep snow. The technique can be the same as that used in compression turns (see page 48) or up unweighted parallels. The main problem – as ever – is starting. Unfortunately, deep snow will cause a drag which means you will be skiing on a steeper slope than you may necessarily have encountered before. Start off with small turns out of the fall line, balancing your weight evenly over both skis. Do not sit back. You must start by pointing your skis almost directly downhill; a traverse position will give you neither the speed nor rhythm to turn.

Whatever parallel techniques you use, it may take a while to get the feel of it. Help yourself by exaggerating all movements strongly. Goggles are a must, as small particles of snow fly everywhere.

GLOSSARY

Angulation A forward bending at the hips, as the upper body tends to follow the momentum when the legs are turned to steer the skis.

Basic swing Rhythmically linked turns with ploughed and skidded phases, which are used to learn the essential elements of parallel skiing.

Cable car In German: Luftseilbahn; in French: Télépherique; in Italian: Funivia. Uphill transport consisting of a cabin suspended from an overhead cable.

Camber The arch that is built into the ski enabling the skier's weight to be distributed along the entire running surface of the ski.

Chair lift In German: Sesselbahn; in French: Télésiège; in Italian: Seggiovia. Uphill transport consisting of double or single seater chairs suspended from an overhead cable. Skis can be worn or carried.

Check A sudden, short skid, to check speed or in preparation for a turn.

Christiania (Christie) A turn made with skis parallel. Named after the place now called Oslo in Norway.

Clock or star turn A method of changing direction on the flat. Its name derives from the pattern left in the snow after a turn is completed.

Compression turns In German: Wellen; in French: Avalement; in Italian: Assorbamento. A turning technique in which the legs are turned whilst bending and extending to keep a constant pressure between the soles of the skis and the snow.

Drag lift An overhead cable system with attachments by which skiers are pulled up a slope. Variations are the poma or button lift, and the T-bar designed for two persons to travel side by side.

Edging The lateral tilting of the skis towards the slope. Used to control the sideways movement of the skis.

Fall line The imaginary line which follows the steepest gradient of a slope.

Foot steer The sensation of steering the ski with the foot, when the leg is rotated around an axis which passes through the ball of the foot.

GLM Graduated Length Method. A method of ski teaching using short skis at first and progressing to longer skis as ability improves. Ski Evolutif is a similar method developed in France.

Herringbone A climbing step with skis in a V-shape open at the tips. The name derives from the pattern left in the snow.

Kick turn Changing direction through 180° in a standing position across a slope.

Linked turns Continuous turning down a slope where one turn leads straight into the next.

Moguls Large rounded bumps on the ski slope formed sometimes by the terrain under the snow but usually by the action of many skiers turning repeatedly in the same place.

Parallel skiing Edges are changed simultaneously, whilst turning and skis are parallel throughout the descent.

Piste Marked and prepared ski run.

Release bindings The mechanisms which secure the boot to the skis. They are designed to release the boots at a pre-determined pressure. The adjustments which determine the point of release must be made in relation to the skill, weight, strength and size of the skier.

Schuss Straight running down the fall line with skis parallel.

Short swings Used on steeper terrain; short quick turns with pronounced edge set helping to control downhill speed.

Side skid A sideways movement of the skis when edged and turned across the direction of the momentum of the skier.

Side slip A sideways movement of the skis due to release of edges and the pull of gravity.

Side stepping A climbing step with skis on their uphill edges horizontally across the fall line.

Ski patrol The organisation responsible for policing the ski area. They are concerned with safety on the pistes, ambulancing and directing ski traffic.

Slalom Controlled downhill skiing between gates. These are pairs of red and blue flags. Giant slalom is a faster version of special slalom.

Snowplough Basic skiing technique with skis held in a V-shape, heels apart and skidding against the inside edges.

Stem Action of moving one ski from a parallel position to an angled position. Movement which enables a skier to start an elementary turn, from a traverse or diagonal skid.

Traverse Movement across a slope holding a line.

Unweighting Moving the body in relation to the skis to bring about a reduction of weight between skis and snow. Unweighting facilitates edge change and turning the skis.

Wedeln Continuous rhythmical linked turns close to the fall line with very little edge set.

INDEX

Page references in bold refer to illustrations.